Once Upon a Whoopee

To: Linda

I hope you have as much fun
reading about the old Macon
Whoopees as we had writing
about them. Thanks for your
support.

Best wishes
Ed Geisamane
October 1998

Once Upon a Whoopee

A Town, A Team,
A Song, A Dream

Ed Grisamore and Bill Buckley

Mercer University Press
Macon, Georgia
1998

©1998

Mercer University Press

6316 Peake Road

Macon, Georgia 31210

All rights reserved.

∞The paper used in this publication meets the minimum requirements
of American National Standard for Permanence of Paper for Printed
Library Materials ANSI Z39.48–1984.

Library of Congress Cataloging-in-Publication Data

Grisamore, Ed and Buckley, Bill

Once upon a whoopee: a town, a team, a song, a dream / Ed
Grisamore and Bill Buckley.

p. cm.

ISBN 0-86554-625-8 (alk. paper)

1. Macon Whoopees (Hockey Team) — History. I. Grisamore, Ed.
II. Title.

GV848.M33B83 1998

796.962′64′09758552 — dc21

98-38041

CIP

TABLE OF CONTENTS

To KeKe,
now high-sticking with the angels

Acknowledgments

The authors wish to express appreciation to our families for putting up with all those long days and short nights working on this book project, many times with different versions of "Makin' Whoopee" playing in the background.

We would like to thank our employers, *The Macon Telegraph*, and Julian Mohr, president of Momar, Inc., for their support and enthusiasm for the book. Also, the *Telegraph* and the archives at the Washington Memorial Library in Macon for their wonderful resources.

Tony McMichael, who drew the original logo and caricature of Mr. Whoopee, was gracious to give us permission to use his material in the design of *Once Upon a Whoopee*. The front-office staff of the new Macon Whoopee, also has given considerable support to the project.

A special thanks to Jane Mortson for setting up a reunion in North Bay, Ontario, in March 1998, and to all the family, friends, and former players who attended.

A big pat on the back to Marc Jolley, our editor at Mercer University Press, who has had a grin on his face from the first day we started talking about writing this story.

And a giant thank you to the good people of Macon and Middle Georgia for maintaining a curious interest for twenty-five years in an unforgettable team.

Another bride, another June
Another sunny honeymoon.
Another season, another reason,
For makin' Whoopee.

A lot of shoes, a lot of rice,
The groom is nervous, he answers twice,
It's really killin', that he's so willin'
to make Whoopee!

Blame It On Doris

Why would anyone pick Macon, Georgia, as the home for a professional ice hockey team?

Because the mayor was a big fan? Nope.

Because of the large, French-speaking, Canadian population in Middle Georgia? Yeah, right.

Because Maconites were sick and tired of going to church on Wednesday and Sunday nights and wanted another way to spend their time? You've got to be kidding.

Actually, the heart of the issue ran right through the Mason-Dixon line. It was the old North versus South squabble. Territorial rights.

St. Petersburg, Fla., Charlotte, N.C., and Greensboro, N.C., were the southern components of the old Eastern Hockey League. And they grew weary of those road trips to the northern venues. They simply didn't want to buy that much diesel for the bus, so they began thinking of ways they could break away and form their own league.

They dreamed of establishing new hockey towns in the South. But the hunt for homes for franchises was limited to cities with an ice facility along a major interstate.

So, that's it. Macon had ice and I-75 running through its front and back door.

It truly was in the right place at the right time.

But there's more to it than that—a lot more.

And if you're thinking all this is Doris Day's fault for singing a gushy version of the old Gus Kahn hit "Makin' Whoopee," you're only partly correct.

Doris certainly deserves an "assist" for playing on the emotions of a thirty-seven-year old stockbroker who was hopelessly in love with her.

She didn't really know it, of course. She just sang the song.

Que Sera, Sera, Whatever Will Be, Will Be,

It was a fine spring evening in Manhattan. Bob Fierro was sitting high above Madison Avenue, looking out the office window of his public relations agency. His creative thought process was shattered by the ringing of his desk telephone.

"Mr. Fierro?" It was Jerry Pinkerton, a stockbroker from Atlanta he had met through a mutual friend.

"Yes, Jerry." Fierro thought Pinkerton was calling for suggestions for where to take a date for dinner in Manhattan.

"They want me to take the hockey team in Macon," said Pinkerton.

"Who wants you to take the team in Macon?"

"You know, Munchak and the guys."

Tedd Munchak was a carpet magnate from North Georgia and the owner of the Carolina Cougars of the American Basketball Association. He also owned the Greensboro Generals hockey team and had been appointed commissioner of the newly formed Southern Hockey League.

Fierro had been hired by the league to research and suggest sites for possible franchises. He had put Macon at the top of his list.

Still, he was not impressed with Pinkerton's news.

"So?"

"Well, should we do it?"

"Look, you've always wanted to be in sports. You're a hockey nut. Form a syndicate and buy the team."

"What would I name it?"

Time stood still. The birds stopped singing. Somewhere, the angels wept as hundreds of lives, relationships, and financial fortunes were about to be changed forever.

Fierro said the name literally came right off the top of his head.

We really should have a moment of silence here.

"I don't know. Why don't you call it the Macon Whoopees?"

There was, according to Fierro, a pregnant pause. "And then a twitter," he said. "I had no idea Jerry's favorite song was Doris Day's recording of 'Makin' Whoopee.'"

Fierro remembers the moment like it happened yesterday. It was like instant recall of where you were the day John F. Kennedy was shot and Neil Armstrong walked on the surface of the moon.

"Although I didn't realize it at the time, Jerry obviously was in love with the idea, and when I dropped the name on him...that did it," Fierro said.

After a moment, the creative part of Madison Avenue was given a chance to start breathing again. It was a momentous occasion.

Pinkerton spoke again. He never said he loved the name, or even liked it. He just gave Fierro an order: "Meet me at the Dallas Cowboy in thirty minutes."

The Dallas Cowboy was a Manhattan watering hole for jocks, media types, and anyone wanting to check his brain at the door.

Fierro disobeyed the order.

"I had a business to run," he said. "I didn't have time for this."

Within a half hour, a very excited Pinkerton was back on the phone with Fierro.

He had asked the maître'd of the bar, Pete Pesce, what he would name a hockey team in Macon, Ga. Pesce suggested the "Macon Eggs."

Pinkerton then found Tim Ryan, the celebrated hockey play-by-play announcer. Ryan was a rising star with NBC and had just signed to broadcast the National Hockey League. Obviously, Ryan's opinion would carry considerable weight with a jock like Pinkerton. Remember now, all the brains are at the door.

"Jerry asked Ryan what he would call a hockey team in Macon," said Fierro. "Ryan thought for a moment and came up with the Macon Eggs as well. At that point, Jerry dropped the name Macon Whoopees on him and shared his idea to own the team."

Said Ryan: "You do that, and I'll announce your scores on national television. I'll make you the Slippery Rock of professional hockey."

Well, the combination of already wondering if he could get Doris Day to sing on opening night and hearing Ryan's barstool promise to take him to new levels of hockey heaven was about all it took.

Great name, no doubt about it. Years later, it would be said that the Macon Whoopees were built on a dream and a song.

It was his dream of Doris, a little whoopee, and his obsession with a song that clearly distracted Pinkerton that night.

"Tim was a sportscaster for the 11 o'clock news on Channel 2 in New York," said Pinkerton. "He told me: 'Be sure and watch tonight.' At the end of his report, he told everybody to sit back and he said: 'There's going to be a hockey team in Macon, Ga., and the name of it is going to be the Macon Whoopees.' Then he signed off."

The weatherman, Frank Field, came on next and asked: "The Macon Whoopees?"

"By that time, what else could I do?" asked Pinkerton.

He called Fierro back from the pay phone.

"I'm going to do it."

Then Fierro asked the question he had the responsibility to ask. It was the question his expertise in looking at financial statements and keeping books had taught him. It was the question that came from the Fierro who had not whimsically popped the name. It was the question from the Fierro who knew black ink from red ink.

"Where are you going to get the money?"

Pinkerton said: "I dunno."

"I was instantly a little nervous," said Fierro. "I felt like I was being included in this. I mean, I had done a business plan for the Southern Hockey League. I told Jerry that it was going to cost him $25,000 to get in and $300,000 a year to operate the team. I said to Jerry again, 'Where are you going to get the money?' He said to me he would go out and raise it."

At that point, Fierro wished Pinkerton luck and hung up, confident he was not involved in any game plans for Macon.

Meanwhile, back at the Charlotte airport, there was a "league meeting." (When you don't have a league office, you hold your meetings in airports.)

"At the airport meeting, they announced that they had awarded Jerry Pinkerton the franchise but he hadn't put up the money yet," said Fierro. "So I went into a room at the airport where Munchak had asked me to meet with him."

"Look," Munchak said to Fierro, "we gave him (Pinkerton) the franchise. He doesn't have any money; he's going to have to go out and raise it. He doesn't even have the $25,000 to put up for the franchise fee."

Fierro was stunned.

"If you agree to take part of the team and to watch him, I'll put up the $25,000 fee," Munchak told Fierro. "I'm going to tell him that you get part of the team."

"Why me?" asked Fierro.

Said Munchak: "Because I need somebody to keep an eye on him. He can't run anything. Get yourself somebody down there to run it. Get yourself twenty-five percent of the team. And that's the way it will be."

The godfather had spoken. Violins were playing in the background. And now Whoopee officially was being made.

Out of wedlock for sure, but that didn't seem to matter.

"The only reason the Macon Whoopees came into being was because Jerry Pinkerton called me and asked me what he should name a hockey team in Macon," said Fierro. "He never considered what he would do for money."

Money. A word that would become a catch phrase for a hockey team—in much the same way the word "iceberg" had special significance for a certain ship on another night to remember.

Just What is a Power Play, Bubba?

Pete Rose had once played baseball in a stadium located just a long fly ball across the river at Luther Williams Field.

Duane Allman had once played his guitar up the hill on Cotton Avenue. Otis Redding had once played "Sittin' On The Dock of the Bay" just a few feet from the front door.

But could Ray Adduno "play" on the frozen floor of the Macon Coliseum?

No one really knew for sure.

The Ice Age officially arrived in Macon on the Fourth of July. The temperature outside the Monument Room was nearing a numeric hat trick in Fahrenheit.

It was a hot day for a wedding, but the vows were exchanged anyway.

For better, for worse. For richer, for poorer. In sickness and in health. 'Til death do us part. But just what is a power play, Bubba?

For Southerners, ice was something you put in your tea, not on a concrete slab. A Bobby Orr? That must be something you stick in your boat when you go fishin'.

Football was king here. Baseball was a close second. Auto racing had its loyal legion of gearheads. And wrasslin' fans traditionally would pack the Coliseum to watch a bunch of guys in tights with names like "Assassin."

Hockey was a foreign sport in the South. They played it up north to give those Yankees something to do when the cold winters forced them inside. Sure, hockey combined the thrills, spills, hitting, spitting, and everything else Southerners liked served with their sports. But would it get good reviews in the hometown of Machine Gun Ronnie?

In 1973, Macon was a city of 122,876 people, 175 churches, sixty schools, four colleges, two television stations, seven radio stations, 177 industries, six hospitals, three downtown bridges, twenty-five restaurants, four banks, and one potential hockey team.

There was a choice of eight state roads and seven federal highways leading you into Macon. No one was quite sure how many of those roads would let you back out.

Of course, some people just waved as they scooted around on the bypass.

"Every time I would drive through Macon, I would start humming that Doris Day song," said Pinkerton. "The name was the only reason I did it. You don't think I would have done it for any other reason, do you?"

Ronnie Thompson, the city's colorful mayor, wasn't so much concerned about all this makin' whoopee as he was makin' money. The giant Coliseum, with 10,000 seats for everything from Elvis concerts to Southern Baptist conventions, had opened during the first year of Thompson's administration in 1968.

It sat across the banks of the Ocmulgee River. Thompson was determined there should never be unsightly vacant spaces in the parking lot. Something had to be done to combat those lonely winter nights when the building was an empty shell of inactivity.

"We knew we had to have some events in the Coliseum because it would break us if we didn't," Thompson said. "Here we were going to have this ice floor, which was all part of the program. Ice skating activities were going to be a mainstay. That's when we started talking about hockey."

Overtures to bring a franchise to Macon began as early as May, 1968, when Tom Lockhart, president of the Eastern Hockey League, expressed an interest in locating a team at the new Coliseum.

The league, which had been in operation since 1933, had a Northern and Southern Division. Charlotte, the first city in the South to introduce hockey seven years earlier, was the mainstay of the Southern Division. Greensboro, N.C., Jacksonville, Fla., Salem, Va., and Nashville, Tenn., also played in the division. But the Nashville franchise was looking to pull out, creating an opening, and the league was shopping around to adopt another city.

After visiting Macon, Lockhart recommended the city wait

another year before bidding on a team. The Coliseum wasn't scheduled to be completed until the Fall, anyway. It would be too much of a rush job. Instead, the Jacksonville team agreed to play several games in Macon during the season.

Bill Lavery, the Coliseum manager, knew all about Jacksonville. He had been the manager there, too, and had opened both the Jacksonville Coliseum and Auditorium when they were built. He had grown up around hockey. He had once managed the Cleveland Arena in Ohio. He even met his wife, Carol, at a hockey game.

"He was a promoter, a show biz guy, a carnival barker," said Thompson.

But could he sell hockey? By October, 1968, Lavery had arranged a game between the Jacksonville Rockets and the Nashville Dixie Flyers. A crowd of 2,000 showed up for what was the first professional hockey game ever played in Georgia.

Thompson became a footnote in history, too. He dropped the ceremonial first puck.

By the next May, Lavery still was trying to test the ice for an entry in the Eastern Hockey League. There were some doubts that the city could pull together a local ownership group to financially back the team. Lavery also was seeking to determine whether the local interest was strong enough to support a team on a regular basis.

Hockey would have to wait another four years before the Whoopees skated their way into Macon's stream of unconsciousness.

A year earlier, the Atlanta Flames had premiered the Ice Age in Georgia. The Flames sold 10,000 season tickets and averaged nearly 13,000 fans per game in the Omni. Macon couldn't be *that* far behind. After all, it was situated on the same stretch of interstate. For gosh sakes, it was in the same time zone.

Lavery was desperate. He wanted to put some seats in those seats. "I needed something to fill in those days," he said. "I knew hockey would take care of about forty dates. What else could you get that could fill forty dates? There was no other attraction out there. An ice show would come in for three days, and the circus might come in for four, but that was it. We knew that if we could get hockey, we would be in pretty good shape."

The obligatory red flag went up for some. Could high-sticking sell tickets in a town of old homes and long drawls, where old men still played checkers under shade trees and little old ladies baked tea cakes for the neighbors on Thursday afternoons?

Even the local newspaper, *The Macon Telegraph*, surmised: "Trying to sell ice hockey in the South is like trying to unload surfboards on Eskimos."

"We knew *we* loved the sport," said Carol Lavery. "Hockey had plenty of action. The diehards were going to come and support a team. Ice skating had done fairly well. People had come and tried it.

"To me, yes, why not? In the Deep South? Well, we would just have to wait and see."

The Grass is Always Greener in a Blue VW

Bill Buckley's parents were just a little worried about their son, the recent college graduate, when they left for a vacation in June, 1973.

"Bill had a very active senior year," explained his mother, Evelyn. "After doing all of the publicity for Guilford College, writing for the newspaper, and broadcasting football and basketball games, he suddenly graduated and things just stopped. He didn't seem very happy."

"I think Bill wanted to do something in sports. He just didn't know what," added Bill Sr. "You can imagine how shocked we were to call home from Williamsburg, Va., and find out that our son was gone. He had gotten a call about a job in Macon, Georgia, borrowed $20 from his sister for gas, and set out driving. He just left. No good-bye. Nothing.

"All I could find out was there was a new sports venture starting up in Macon, and he had an interview. I remember thinking: 'What kind of pro sport do they play in Macon, Georgia?' The more we thought about it, the more concerned we became."

Buckley had been cutting the grass at his parents' house in Greensboro. He had gone indoors to enjoy a little air conditioning when the phone rang. It was Norman Curtis, an official with the local hockey team, the Greensboro Generals.

No, Curtis still didn't have a job opening. But he told Buckley about a position in Macon where a new franchise had been awarded. Macon needed a publicity guy, and Curtis had given Buckley's name to Pinkerton. Pinkerton wanted to talk to the young college grad. Buckley couldn't move fast enough. He never finished mowing the grass.

After taking a shower and packing for the trip, Buckley felt he needed to leave immediately. He was afraid that if he didn't get on the road at once, someone else might get *his* job.

Buckley told his younger sister, Kathy, that he was off for a job interview. She asked if he had any idea how to get to Macon. He didn't. They located the family atlas. There was Macon, just south of Atlanta. Buckley had never been to Atlanta. In fact, the farthest south he had ever driven was to South Carolina.

With his sister's $20 in his pocket, Buckley started out of the driveway in the baby blue Volkswagen he had purchased just prior to his senior year. Suddenly he remembered he had a hockey stick in the garage. He had it when he played junior hockey and figured he might need a hockey stick if he got the job.

After finding it between two rakes and a shovel in the utility room, Buckley tried to position it into the car. No matter what the angle, he could not make it fit. Finally, he opened the sunroof and stuck it through. The blade hung a foot out of the top of the VW roof, but at least it was accompanying him to Macon.

Two hours later, he passed through Charlotte on I-85. He was beyond excited. He suddenly realized that he never had asked the name of the hockey team. He always had been a Greensboro Generals fan and worried about how he would feel when the Macon team played his beloved Generals.

Farther down I-85, at a rest stop in Spartanburg, S.C., Buckley started wondering if he knew enough about ice hockey to do a good job. He remembered how long the month of June had seemed with so few interviews.

Perhaps, after looking so hard for a job, the job just may have found him. Still, there was a little disappointment. The Guilford basketball team had won a national small college championship in March with future NBA stars M.L. Carr and Lloyd "World B." Free on its roster. Buckley would have preferred a job with a basketball team. After all, he was a North Carolina product, and roundball was his love.

As he reached Greenville, S.C., mild anxiety set in. Buckley realized that he never had been south of where he was now. He stopped to check the map—just to make sure Atlanta was still where it was supposed to be.

Later that night, Buckley arrived in Atlanta and met Jerry Pinkerton for his "interview."

Buckley was all set to tell the Macon team owner about his experience in college. He had written press releases and developed brochures. He had left home in too much of a hurry to remember to bring any examples of his work, but he had a mental list of all the things he could do for a sports team. He was oozing with enthusiasm and ready for any question.

But the questions never came. Not one.

Pinkerton bought Buckley a beer and then another. He told the recent college graduate about a guy named KeKe Mortson he had hired to manage and coach the team. KeKe was a hero of Pinkerton's. He had idolized Mortson when KeKe had been a player in Hershey, Pennsylvania.

After talking about KeKe and giving Buckley the "play-by-play" account about the creation of the Macon Whoopees, Pinkerton bought another beer and asked, laughing, "So, you want to join this outfit?"

Buckley had made that decision before he ever made the call to Pinkerton. The two of them headed to the Atlanta airport to pick up the legendary KeKe Mortson who was due in on a 10 P.M. flight from Toronto.

Within twenty-four hours, the owner, the publicity guy, and the coach were headed to Macon to be introduced to the local media as the new management team of the new game in town. Pinkerton had arranged for a press conference. Yesterday, Buckley was cutting the grass. Today, he was cutting a spot for the local radio sports show.

Buckley had been around the media his entire college career. His job at Guilford had included everything from arranging interviews for the local TV station and providing weekly statistics to the newspaper to providing coffee and sandwiches in the press box during football games. He always was *behind* the camera. If his name was in the paper, it was a by-line on a story he had written.

Now, he was the one being photographed, and he was the one being interviewed. He had the job of his dreams. He was afraid to pinch himself.

Several days later, Buckley finally called his father back in Greensboro.

His dad asked a perfectly logical question. Anyone who had

just taken a job should have been able to answer it.

"How much are you going to be paid?"

Buckley couldn't answer. In all of the excitement, the subject of his salary just hadn't come up.

Field Goalies and
Pigskin Pucks

Inside the cinder-block restaurant, Pinkerton pushed aside a plate of fried chicken, gripped the podium with both hands, and got ready to deliver his locker-room speech.

Where was he? Hawkinsville?

What was this? The Kiwanis Club?

It made no difference. This was another reason, another preseason, for talking Whoopee.

He did know this much: He was below the gnat line and somewhere near the goal line.

Pinkerton was on foreign soil, stumping through any small south Georgia town within an hour's drive of Macon that would put him on the program as the guest speaker for Monday's civic club meeting. Out in the hinterlands, he knew he would have to interpret this game to audiences who thought the Stanley Cup was something Homer Stanley spit in when he pulled out a wad of chewing tobacco.

If Pinkerton was going to sell a Yankee cookie to a bunch of crackers, he would have to throw deep to win their approval. Maybe it was time to call an audible, he thought. He was smack dab in the middle of the smash-mouth South, where entire towns routinely empty themselves into high school football stadiums every Friday night.

Football isn't just a sport in Southern climes. It is a religious experience. It is Saturday pilgrimages between the hedges in Athens and over on the plains of Auburn. It has been known to consume entire calendars with the four seasons—preseason, regular season, spring practice, and recruiting season.

The history and emotional connection between the South and football is so pronounced that grown men have barked, cried, lived, and died on the performances of 19-year-old sophomores from places like Valdosta and Wrightsville.

Pinkerton looked out and sized up his all-male audience—

these self-proclaimed Southerners by the grace of God. They might not be able to tell you what size dress their wives wear, but they could recite heights, weights, rushing statistics, and the number of tackles posted by every member of Vince Dooley's incoming freshman class at Georgia.

It was time to buckle his chinstrap and draw up the play.

"Boys," he said, "if they didn't keep score, they'd call it war."

This was the game plan. No one said educating the public was going to be easy.

It wasn't enough to have to scout players, arrange travel, book practice times, and print tickets. The front office of the Whoopees found itself spending considerable time preaching and teaching the game to a fan base that was, for the most part, slap-shot illiterate.

"Nobody really knew what the sport was about," Whoopee defenseman Mike Penasse would later say. "That was very unusual for us. Coming from Canada, you live it every day. It's hockey, hockey, hockey."

But this clearly was not hockey turf. The Whoopees soon realized that evoking comparisons to football would be their salvation. Had anyone thought of it, having KeKe Mortson wear a houndstooth cap might have been a good public relations ploy. Can Bear Bryant really walk on water, er, ice?

"The first couple of civic club meetings were really dull," said Buckley. "We showed a film that explained the rules and a player demonstrated putting on the equipment. The members looked bewildered. People were talking, and lots of plates, silverware, and glasses were clinking. Those people were not spellbound by what we had to say."

That's when the Whoopees realized football references were their ticket to a disinterested public. "We started seeing brighter, understanding faces when we began to relate hockey rules to football rules," Buckley said. "No one understood icing, but they did understand when we called it 'intentional grounding.' Offsides and the blue line made more sense when we used the football comparison to offsides. I'm not sure we ever made any progress with the penalty box. That didn't fit anywhere in football."

Civic clubs weren't the only targets of remedial hockey lessons. The Whoopees tutored schools, church groups, and sororities. They wasted no chance to bend ears and open minds.

"I don't know much about promoting, but I do know people," said KeKe. "When you're at these civic club meetings and they laugh, you laugh. When they clap, you clap."

The Whoopees' traveling classroom was a hit in the schools. Robert McDuffie, who went on to become one of the nation's top violinists and a Grammy nominee, was a high school student when the Whoopees showed up for an orientation at Macon's First Presbyterian Day School.

"They told us that they had this blond-headed goon on the Whoopees. He was supposed to be the star of the team and to look for him because he liked to start fights," McDuffie said. "They also mentioned that the Macon Whoopees had been a question on the TV show *Hollywood Squares*."

So Pinkerton figured that the old notion, "I went to a fight and a hockey game broke out" couldn't hurt either. One of the early players brought in was Blake Ball, a rock 'em, sock 'em player who had a reputation for taking off the gloves for a bare-fisted brawl.

The Whoopees also tried to draw blood with the professional wrestling crowd. But there was a fine blue line to be walked there: How to ignite the loyal wrasslin' masses without sacrificing the legitimacy of hockey.

"We got a lot of questions asking whether the fighting was real," Buckley said. "We struggled to explain how the blood on the ice came from a body—not a capsule filled with food coloring."

The awareness campaign by Pinkerton and others did not go unnoticed and unappreciated by the local press. Harley Bowers, sports editor of *The Macon Telegraph*, wrote that Pinkerton's enthusiasm was becoming contagious.

"He's not demanding anything from anybody," Bowers said. "He's not begging. He tells the story of his hockey venture in simple, interesting language. He promises, in fact guarantees, excitement. All he requests from his listeners is that they try his product."

The efforts never stopped. They rarely slowed down. One day, Buckley took the hockey stick he had brought with him from Greensboro and walked through downtown Macon.

"I was trying to see what kind of reaction I would get," he said. "I had to explain to some people how it was held—which end!"

If that didn't provide an indication of how much work still lay ahead, the affirmation came in the design and planning of the game program. It wasn't so much a souvenir program as it was an instruction manual.

Included in the forty-eight pages were reams of copy about hockey rules, history, hockey terms, signs and infractions, and cartoon descriptions of the different positions. There were articles on the speed of the game, the different zones on the ice, and a two-page spread on "How to be a Fan."

"It wasn't a hockey program, it was a primer," said Buckley. "We should have paid the fans to read it, not sell it to them."

Write from Left Field

The words came. They never flowed, but at least they were there. In the air. On the printed page.

Even though Harley Bowers was considered the dean of Georgia sportswriters, he always was looking over his shoulder when he sat down to tell *Telegraph* readers about hockey. It was as if he were hoping some great Zamboni of journalism would come behind him to help smooth the ice.

"When it came to hockey, I really didn't have a clue what I was writing about," said Bowers. "But at least most of the people who were reading it didn't have a clue either."

Bowers didn't profess to be an expert, nor did he particularly want to be. The *Telegraph's* readership never had demanded that the local sports section run the scores and standings from the National Hockey League and World Hockey Association on a daily basis. There wasn't enough interest warrant the space.

There were some neophyte hockey fans with the arrival of the NHL's Atlanta Flames a year earlier. But, in Macon, hockey coverage traditionally was an afterthought—a plug to fill empty spaces on slow days or fodder for large newsholes.

When the Whoopees hit town, there were twelve cable channels and two local network affiliates available in Macon. (These were the days before ESPN, CNN, Fox, and the SuperStation.) So having only a dozen stations to flip through didn't really matter. Few people had cable anyway. Or remotes.

And Bowers knew it wasn't a prerequisite that he become an authority on the Southern Hockey League. After all, he was the sports editor. He could assign someone else on his staff to cover the Whoopees beat.

Ellis Pope didn't exactly volunteer. He was, however, recruited.

"Harley called me over to his desk one afternoon and asked

what I knew about hockey," Pope said. "Well, I knew Bobby Orr played for the Boston Bruins, the Detroit Red Wings had a cool-looking logo, and you didn't serve corn-on-the-cob at an NHL picnic."

Good enough. He was "hired."

Another Pope, this one named Bobby and of no relation to Ellis, would sit on the set of Macon's top-rated television station, WMAZ-TV. He tried not to make it too obvious that he had a limited working knowledge of the game.

"I didn't know a blue line from a hockey puck," said Bobby Pope. "There wasn't that much hockey on television at that time, except for maybe the Stanley Cup playoffs. We didn't have a lot to compare it with because it was basically an Eastern and Canadian sport."

It was as if an alien spacecraft had descended on Macon and dropped dozens of creatures onto the ice. Who were these toothless wonders? Better yet, did anybody care?

Said Bobby Pope: "I knew an offsides was similar to the offsides in football, but it took me a while to learn about icing and high-sticking. I really didn't know what I was talking about half the time."

If Bobby Pope was challenged to report hockey to his viewers, Ellis Pope had equal expectations when filing daily stories on his newspaper beat. At least he had somewhat of an advantage. He had watched some hockey when he was in the Marine Corps stationed in Maryland.

"It was all over the sports pages there, so I had some knowledge of teams and a few players," he said. "But that was about all. I had no knowledge of the rules. I didn't know you could be offsides without smashing a defensive tackle in the mouth. And, somehow crossing the red line and blue line was not nearly as exciting as crossing the goal line."

A few days before the season opener, the *Telegraph* and its afternoon counterpart, *The Macon News*, ran full pages of previews, including detailed stories explaining how the game was played.

Although his sports staff was committed to covering the team, Bowers had what he called "grave doubts" that hockey would catch on from the very beginning.

"I don't think there has ever been a better nickname than the Macon Whoopees," he said. "I always have been anxious to see anything succeed in Macon. But I knew it was going to be a hard sell. It was obvious that there was more interest in football and basketball. Hockey was something way out there in…well, out in left field."

As the Whoopees prepared for their debut, Ellis Pope lifted his pen — the newspaper equivalent of high-sticking — and observed.

Many of the well-schooled hockey fans came from nearby Warner Robins, a city about fifteen miles south of Macon. Since World War II, Robins Air Force Base had relocated scores of military families in the area, and many of them eventually had chosen to retire there. These transplants had cut their teeth on ice hockey.

It wasn't difficult to tell them apart from the novices, who could only pretend to understand the finer points of the game.

Said Ellis Pope: "All through the Coliseum, in between spits of Red Man, you could hear: '*Hi stickin', hi stickin'. He wuz hi stickin' ref.*' A well-executed deke on a defenseman or a delicate assist on a goal was not easy to appreciate.

"But whomping someone with a stick? Now that was a language most Southerners understood."

Whoop, There It Was

Before there was another bride and another June, there was another tune. Call it a blind date.

It belonged to Werner Janssen, a New York composer and conductor who actually put the original *whoop* into Whoopee.

Years before songwriters Gus Kahn and Walter Donaldson gave the music world the fun and whimsical "Makin' Whoopee" in 1928, Janssen was the brainchild of a song called "Come On, Let's Make Whoopee."

Although it was just one of many Broadway show tunes he wrote for the Ziegfield Follies in the 1920s, it never achieved the notoriety of the song that succeeded it. But it planted the musical seeds that Kahn and Donaldson sowed to bring everlasting whoopee to America's ears.

In its seventy-year history, "Makin' Whoopee" has been played and sung by everyone from Eddie Cantor to Doris Day, Frank Sinatra, Ray Charles, Danny Thomas, Nat King Cole, Judy Garland, Mel Torme, Louie Armstrong, Miles Davis, Count Basie, Gerry Mulligan, and Ella Fitzgerald.

In recent years, the song has been recorded by such artists as Toni Tennille, Ray Stevens, and Harry Nilsson. Actress Michelle Pfeiffer sang it on the soundtrack of the movie, "The Fabulous Baker Boys." Dr. John and Rickie Lee Jones whooped it up with a version in the movie "Sleepless In Seattle," starring Tom Hanks and Meg Ryan.

And, of course, the song has turned up in Cadillac commercials, too.

"When I first heard it in the 1970s, it took me a while to realize they were talking about something else besides a hockey team," said Bill Elder, a popular Macon radio disc jockey. "Look how much our standards have dropped in society. Now they're using the same song to sell a family car on TV!"

Did Werner Janssen have all this in the back seat of his mind?

Well, actually...

21

He met Bruce Lockerbie in Stony Brook, N.Y., in 1973, and the two became such close friends that Lockerbie would begin writing a biography of Janssen's life. That same year, Janssen knocked on Lockerbie's door.

"Here's a strange one," he said, showing his friend a check that had appeared in the mail.

It was a royalty check from ASCAP—the American Society of Composers, Authors and Publishers—for the use of the name "Whoopee."

Curiously enough, it had nothing to do with a song.

"He thought it was quite amusing that he was getting a check through ASCAP for something that was as far from art, at least in his mind, as a professional hockey team," Lockerbie said.

Janssen was such a renowned classical musician that he seemed to be an odd fit for a song about Whoopee. But that's because he chose to pen many of his songs under different names. He wrote musical scores for about fifty films, including "The General Died At Dawn"—an Academy Award winning movie in 1936 starring Gary Cooper.

He was considerably more famous as a conductor and was the first native New Yorker to conduct the New York Philharmonic. He later conducted orchestras in Baltimore, Los Angeles, Salt Lake City, Portland, and San Diego. He was a guest conductor for the Berlin Philharmonic. He was praised for his work in Helsinki, Finland, by one of history's most famous composers, Jean Sibelius.

If his music wasn't enough to make him famous, his 1937 marriage to actress Ann Harding moved him into the spotlight. Harding had been nominated for an Academy Award for best actress in the 1930 film, "Holiday." The couple divorced, and Janssen later remarried. He died in 1990, and Bruce Lockerbie's biography never has been published.

Lockerbie's son, Don, got to know Janssen as a friend of the family growing up in Stony Brook. Don Lockerbie landed his first job out of college in Macon.

He was hired as track coach at Stratford Academy by Henry Tift, his former high school English teacher who had been named headmaster at the Macon private school. (Don Lockerbie later became track coach at his alma mater, the University of North Carolina, and then became a private design consultant for stadiums and tracks all over the world.)

"Werner used to joke about the fact that I lived in Macon and there was a team called the Whoopees," said Don Lockerbie. "He just loved that. He was very proud, but he also couldn't believe the irony of a hockey team in Georgia. He always said he thought that had to be the most unique and original name in sports."

If Janssen was the Thomas Edison of Whoopee, it was Gus Kahn and Walter Donaldson who flipped the switch to the words and music that made generations of music-lovers smile. Together, they became one of the most formidable song-writing teams of their era, and "Makin' Whoopee" became one of their snappiest and most identifiable songs.

A native New Yorker, Donaldson taught himself to play the piano and began composing songs while still in school. He enjoyed early successes with "The Daughter of Rosie O'Grady" and "How Ya Gonna Keep 'Em Down On The Farm?" His major break came when Al Jolson recorded Donaldson's tune "My Mammy." His collaboration with Kahn produced such songs as "I'll See You In My Dreams," "Carolina In the Morning," and "Yes, Sir, That's My Baby."

The German-born Kahn became one of the most prolific lyricists of the 1920s and '30s and worked with such notables as Jolson, George Gershwin, The Marx Brothers, and history's most famous dance team—Fred Astaire and Ginger Rogers. In a trade poll, Kahn once was voted as the nation's second-most popular songwriter behind Irving Berlin.

After Kahn and Donaldson had "Makin' Whoopee" down on paper in 1928, the song became a hit record after it was sung by Eddie Cantor in the Broadway show "Whoopee." Two years later, Cantor sang it in "Whoopee," a 94-minute film produced by Samuel Goldwyn and Florenz Ziegfeld Jr.

It was an early Technicolor musical starring Cantor as a hypochondriac whose move out West for health reasons results in a series of calamities. It was nominated for an Oscar in 1932 for Best Art Direction (Richard Day).

Between the Broadway play and the movie was, of course, the

start of something history calls the "Great Depression."

Cantor later sang "Makin' Whoopee" in the movie, "Show Business" in 1940 and it was included on the soundtrack from "The Eddie Cantor Story" in 1953. Cantor put a personal twist on the first line of the song, substituting "groom" for "June" in "Another bride, another June." Other artists followed Cantor's lead.

Kahn died in 1941 at the age of 54. Ten years after his death, the movie, "I'll See You In My Dreams," was based on his life story. Actor Danny Thomas played the role of Kahn. Kahn's wife, composer Grace LeBoy, was played by Doris Day.

When Thomas and Day sang the song, "Makin' Whoopee," the song officially was reincarnated a generation later. It was the fabulous 1950s—a decade that would change America with the invention of the computer chip and birth-control pill, and the advent of television, commercial airline travel, and the interstate highway system.

Ace Azar, a cousin of Danny Thomas, was a well-known entertainer who owned a nightclub called the "Tropics" on Cotton Avenue in Macon in the 1940s and '50s. He did stand-up comedy at the Tropics, and, when "I'll See You In My Dreams" began playing around the corner at the Ritz Theater, he wrote a parody of the Makin' Whoopee song for his floor show. To the same tune, he would sing:

> *My cousin is playing, down at the Ritz*
> *The show's terrific, it's sure a hit*

Azar moved from Macon to Hollywood in 1952 and began appearing in a number of situation comedies, including "The Andy Griffith Show," "Make Room For Daddy," "I Dream of Jeanie," and "Gomer Pyle." He also had nightclub acts in Los Angeles, Las Vegas and Chicago. Two decades later, while returning to Macon to visit his father and brother, Azar sat by a young man on the plane while flying from Chicago to Atlanta.

"We started talking, and I asked him what he did for a living and where he was going," Azar said. "He told me he was a hockey player and he was headed to Macon, Georgia.

"And I said: 'You're going to Macon to play hockey?' I had lived in Macon, of course. When he told me the name of the team was the Macon Whoopees, I sang him a couple of lines of the song. But he was too young to remember it."

The hockey player who was headed to Macon was Brian Tapp. He was flying to Atlanta where he would meet Whoopees officials for the ride to Macon.

"When this guy heard I was going to play for the Macon Whoopees, he started talking about some song Doris Day had sung. I had never heard the song. Then he started singing, right there on the airplane! I really thought he was full of it. Now I know he was telling the truth."

In December 1973, at the offices of the Gus Kahn Music Company on Selma Avenue in Hollywood, Donald Kahn was old enough to remember. A friend stopped by and gave him a Macon Whoopees decal. The son of Gus Kahn was thrilled, and he wrote the team a letter.

> *We wanted you to know that although we are many miles away from you, we are with you in spirit. (We) hope on behalf of yourselves, the song and the memory of my late father that you have a most successful season.*

MAKIN' WHOOPEE
Words and Music by Gus Kahn and Walter Donaldson

Another bride, another June
Another sunny honeymoon
Another season, another reason
For Makin' Whoopee.

A lot of shoes, a lot of rice
The groom is nervous, he answers twice
It's really killin', that he's so willin'
To make whoopee!

Picture a little love nest

Down where the roses cling,
Picture the same sweet love nest,
Think what a year can bring.

He's washing dishes and baby clothes
He's so ambitious, he even sews
But don't forget, folks, that's what you get, folks,
For Makin' Whoopee!

Another year, or maybe less
What's this I hear? Well, can't you guess?
She feels neglected, and he's suspected
Of Makin' Whoopee!

She sits alone. most every night
He doesn't phone, he doesn't write
He says he's busy, but she says "is he?"
He's Makin' Whoopee!

He doesn't make much money
Only five-thousand per
Some judge, who thinks he's funny
Told him he got to pay six to her

He says: "Now judge, suppose I fail."
The judge says: "Budge, right into jail!
You'd better keep her, I think it's cheaper
Than Makin' Whoopee!!"

I Couldn't Play
the Violin, Anyway

He came from a religious home, but the ice was his sanctuary. The quiet Sunday mornings in Kirkland Lake, Ontario, were roused by the sound of KeKe Mortson's skates.

"Our mother was very religious," said Mortson's brother, Dennis. "We had to go to church every Sunday—except for KeKe. KeKe was excused. He didn't have to come with us. He went to the ice rink instead."

It was just one of the first signs of KeKe's being one of life's unique people. He had an exemption from church.

While Dennis was on his knees, KeKe was on his skates. KeKe would lace up his skates in the family home and then walk, skates and all, to the neighborhood's outdoor rink.

"The rink was surrounded by a wooden fence," said Dennis. "KeKe would pick out a knot in the boards, and he would skate as hard as he could from one end to the other and then shoot the puck at the knot—over and over and over."

Sunday morning target practice resulted in more than a few "knocked out knots" and broken boards.

"That created," Dennis laughed, "just a few hassles with the townspeople."

Interestingly enough, some thirty years later, KeKe would head south where he would—once again—skate and shoot while most folks were in church.

Cleland Lindsay Mortson was nicknamed "KeKe" (pronounced Key Key) by his older brother, Vern. "I was about two years old when KeKe came along, and I just couldn't get 'Cleland' out," said Vern. "I got 'Cle' out, and then 'Cle-Cle', and that became KeKe. The other kids in the neighborhood called him that, and the nickname stuck."

And the rest, as they say, is history. Hockey history. There never has been another player with the nickname "KeKe" in all of the records of the game. Just like the hockey team he later would coach, his name was a conversation piece.

"I didn't mind the name," KeKe said. "I couldn't play the violin anyway. And that's about all a name like Cleland fits. My mother named me. Sometimes I think she couldn't have liked me too much."

So, the question becomes: Did Mother Mortson "exempt" KeKe from church because she wanted him to practice his art? Or was it because she didn't want to sit next to him during the service?

His name was just the beginning of his uniqueness. "I don't mean to be different," he once said. "It's just that things keep happening to me that don't happen to other guys."

Not that KeKe had *anything* to do with these "happenings." Like the night he scored a goal on a road trip and answered the boos by feeding the furious home crowd peanuts through the wire fence. Or the night the opposing fans started calling him a dirty old man. KeKe waited between periods so he'd be the last to leave the ice, put his stick under his arm, and limped off the ice as if he were using the stick as a crutch. "The fans liked those things," said KeKe. "So why not do them?"

One night in Buffalo, while playing for the Baltimore Clippers, he started such a fight on the ice that it took 72 policemen to escort his team out of the arena. "I felt like one of those American politicians running for office, " said Mortson. "The Buffalo fans were yelling, 'Give us Mortson!' but I'm happy no one did. I saw a lot of 'Hang Mortson' signs at the games, but it was good for the crowds. We drew about 40,000 for the four games. While I was a bum in Buffalo, the Baltimore reporters gave me the hero treatment in their write-ups. I was even presented with an award as the sweetest guy in Baltimore at one of the games."

Although he never admitted to starting any controversy on the ice, he did always seem to be around it. "All my penalties were good ones," he said. "I always made it a point to take somebody from the other team with me into the penalty box."

While many hockey players spent the off-season relaxing, KeKe returned to North Bay after every hockey season to spend the summer working for the city's sewage treatment plant.

"A hockey player is only as good as his last shift," he said.

"When my playing days are over, my summer-time job will become my full-time job. I am the Norton (Jackie Gleason's sewage-plant working friend—Ed Norton—in *The Honeymooners*) of North Bay."

Co-workers at the plant were so entertained KeKe's antics, they wrote a song about him entitled, "The Ballad of Big Keek."

Colorful? Yes. Unique? Absolutely.

Fined? Well, yes...that, too.

"Don't ever tell KeKe he can't do something," said brother Dennis. "In Quebec, they had a rule. Wearing helmets was mandatory. They should have never told KeKe he had to wear a helmet."

KeKe didn't object to helmets. In fact, he was very much in favor of them. But, because it was a rule, he didn't wear one. Game after game, he was fined.

"Some of those fines really added up," said Dennis. "I did his tax returns. I know. During a few of those seasons, his fines alone added up to more than I was earning in a year."

Later in Dallas, they didn't tell him he had to wear a helmet. He wore one. Of course, it was different. It was red. It was the only red helmet on the team.

Bill Dineen, who later coached KeKe in the World Hockey Association with the Houston Aeros, remembered some extra-curricular practice one year in Quebec.

"KeKe and I used to stay after practice to work on some things," said Dineen. "One night, we stayed longer than usual, and they started turning out the lights at the rink. KeKe told me, 'You gotta learn how to flip the puck,' and he proceeded to flip the puck in the air, bouncing it off the big scoreboard clock that hung over center ice."

The arena manager called KeKe over and "gave him hell," according to Dineen. "The very next day at practice, coach Floyd Curry confronted KeKe with the incident, intending to embarrass him in front of the whole team. KeKe told him: 'All I was trying to do was kill a little time.' That broke everybody up."

KeKe was in Houston for the inaugural season of the WHA. Players like Bobby Hull and Gordie Howe were coming out of retirement from the NHL for the money and excitement of a new league.

When Howe, the infamous No. 9 of the Detroit Red Wings, arrived in Houston, there was already a No. 9, KeKe Mortson. Mortson knew he had to give up his number so, in 1973, long before Gretzky was great, KeKe added a "9" to make "99." He was the first player to wear "99."

"KeKe dealt with everybody at the same level," said Dineen. "Whether it was a Gordie Howe or a kid in his first year in the pros, it didn't matter. Not many people have the ability to do that and get away with it. KeKe could give anybody and everybody a hard time and leave them laughing. They never felt offended."

KeKe could equal the stars on the ice as well. The Winnipeg Jets had lured Bobby Hull out of retirement with a promise of millions. As the Aeros met the Jets, Hull scored a dramatic power play goal to force the game into overtime. But it was KeKe who scored the overtime goal to send the Golden Jet home a loser.

One of the thousands of fans who had watched KeKe play was Jerry Pinkerton. Pinkerton was in high school when KeKe was skating with the Hershey Bears in Hershey, Pa.

"I never missed a game," said Pinkerton, a native of Hershey. "KeKe was the team's center. He was a folk hero. With that shrill voice of his, he would call for the puck by calling his name. He would slap his stick on the ice and yell 'KeKeKeKeKeKe!!' until someone passed it to him.

"In my high school yearbook, it says under my picture that someday I'll own a hockey team and KeKe Mortson will be my coach."

After the first WHA season ended in early 1973, Dineen and KeKe had a talk. "KeKe thought he could still play at the WHA level," said Dineen. "I told him that he was welcome to come back. But, with the younger players we had in Houston, I knew he was probably not going to get as much ice time as he expected. I told him he was going to have to accept that."

"Ice time" was always a key issue with KeKe, and he was accustomed to getting his way. Once, while playing for the Canadian Olympic team, he took himself out of the game after scoring two goals. Although he was just one goal from a coveted hat trick, he was angry with the coach for not giving him more ice time.

Father Time was knocking on KeKe's door. At age thirty-nine, KeKe slammed the door in his face.

"I don't see anything special about playing hockey at my age," he once said. "I stay in condition; I work outdoors and run three miles a day in the off-season. I've always stayed in shape, and I give 100 per cent every minute I'm out there."

He had been asked, many times, about the possibility of coaching a team. But none of those doing the asking was doing any of the offering. Suddenly, the phone rang in Houston where KeKe was pondering his future. It was the old fan from Hershey who was "offering a club."

"I encouraged KeKe to take the Macon team," said Dineen. "I had felt, for some time, he'd make a great coach. But, KeKe really went to Macon because he felt he could still play. He got the most out of whatever ability he had because of his desire. He played all out. He gave the game 100 percent—more than 99 percent of all of the hockey players that ever played the game."

You had to figure Dineen knew what he was talking about. After all, he had played on three Stanley Cup teams with Detroit.

Pinkerton and Buckley walked through the baggage claim area of the Atlanta airport on July 3, 1973. Suddenly, as if he'd seen Elvis, Pinkerton yelled: "KeKe! KeKe Mortson!"

As the three exchanged greetings, KeKe looked at the briefcase Pinkerton was carrying and asked, "You got my money in there?"

He was wearing a checked shirt and striped pants. He looked as if he had dressed in the dark. But, then, KeKe never matched. He walked like a duck and was smoking an obnoxious cigar.

The North Bay Nugget newspaper published a press release from Macon: "The reason behind the signing of Mortson was three-fold: his ability to still play while managing and coaching; his ability to work with the younger players on and off the ice; and the amount of time he put into the sport."

Buckley could recall those words. He had written them down, as KeKe dictated them, the first night they were together.

KeKe was going to coach and manage. Most of all, he was going to continue KeKe's "Escapades On Ice."

"I've never put on a show to hurt my own club," KeKe said. "Basically, everything I do is spontaneous. People will go home from the game and not remember anybody on my club unless it's me. Maybe I've given them something extra, something to bring them back."

As the preseason wound down, KeKe stepped up the activity in practice. The players felt it. Thanks to Ben Gay and aspirin they endured it.

"KeKe was a driver," said rightwinger Al Rycroft, remembering the days before the season began. "He had us in amazing condition."

"KeKe knew how to get a team going," recalled another player, Brian Tapp. "He always expected more of himself than anyone else. If other lines were going down and back four times in practice, his line had to do six. That's just the way it was."

"He wanted you to be in top shape," said defenseman Mike Penasse. "We ran and ran and ran. He pushed us. He pushed himself."

Two days before the season started, KeKe was quoted in the Macon newspaper: "We'll work hard here. I believe one must sweat a little in order to accomplish the job. We will be in good condition. We will enjoy our work. We will win. All I've ever been is a winner. Why stop now?"

In towns across Canada and the U.S., KeKe had endured a lifetime of opening nights under a number of different coaches. Ice time was precious to him, perhaps his most prized possession.

As one of those seasons ended, KeKe was unhappy with the ice time he had gotten during the year. He arrived at the rink and sawed off one end of the wooden bench. He had spent more time on the bench that year than on the ice. "This bench is my memory of this year," he said. "I'll take this part as my souvenir."

On opening night in Macon, everything would be different.

Ice time wouldn't be a problem. This ice was *his* ice.

As he stepped into the rink, KeKe Mortson would be playing for a coach who demanded more of him than any other coach during his entire career.

KeKe would be playing for KeKe.

Want to Buy an Ad in a Hockey Program, Eh?

Wayne Horne absolutely loved his summer job. He would walk into downtown restaurants and other businesses and spread the word about the Macon Whoopees.

"I would show them the size of the ad they could buy in the program," Horne said. "I would tell them they could buy a full-page or half-page or quarter-page ad and how thousands of people would come to the rink and buy the program, and see their ad and how that would increase their business. I got a pretty good reception."

Jerry Pinkerton was a sales manager without a sales team. The product? Hockey. To many Middle Georgians, that was something a bull left behind in a field.

He didn't have a promotion team.

He didn't have a phone.

He did have a hockey player. *One* hockey player.

"Jerry selected me in the league expansion draft from Roanoke in early June," said Horne. "He asked me to come down to Macon. Obviously, he wanted to get hockey going and get the fans to know a little about the game. He wanted me to sell hockey to the folks in Macon. I decided to take him up on his offer.

"My first night in Macon, I checked into the hotel and went for a walk downtown," said Horne. "As I walked through the city, people stared at me. They must have thought I was some kind of crazy guy."

Horne's hair trailed to his shoulders, and he had a "funny" accent for Maconites. Every sentence he spoke ended with the expression "eh?"

One of Wayne's first jobs was to simply skate.

"I would go down to the rink at the Coliseum," he said. "They had public skating, and Jerry wanted me to get out and meet the people. He figured that all the people who were interested in ice

33

skating in June and July would probably be interested in watching a hockey game in October. I was like a showcase of the game. People would ask me questions, and I would answer them. If they wanted me to help them learn to skate, I would help them."

Oh, there were some summer road trips—from one restaurant to another. That's when Pinkerton, Horne, and Buckley rode the civic club circuit. "Jerry would take us to the civic clubs to talk about hockey," Horne said. "I was the only hockey player in town, so I would explain the rules, discuss what the puck was made of, and mention how there were right-handed and left-handed hockey sticks just like golf clubs."

Horne also would talk about the length of the ice, the length of the game, the penalties, and other details of the sport.

So, did any of the businessmen and women at the civic clubs know anything about hockey? "Oh, no," said Horne. "They were very well-dressed business people who knew nothing about hockey. They didn't ask too many questions because they didn't know enough about the game to ask a lot of questions. After I'd speak and let them know some of the terms, they'd ask a few questions and ask me to explain what cross-checking was, what icing was, and why there were two blue lines and one red line on the ice—things like that."

Horne was in hockey heaven. The summer job with Pinkerton was fun and profitable. "Hey, I was making pretty good money for then," he said. "You gotta remember, the $250 per week Jerry was paying me for *talking up* the game was almost as much as I got during the season for *playing* the game!"

And there were no face-offs, no high sticks. Horne does remember being a little scared of the civic clubs. "I never had done anything like that before," said Horne. "I'm not a speaker. I was pretty uncomfortable getting up in front of those big businessmen. But I just told myself: 'Well, I know what I'm talking about, and they don't.' I knew they couldn't argue with me. They didn't know enough to argue."

Back in March of 1973, Wayne Horne had been on the ice with the Roanoke Valley Rebels. The Rebels had won the Southern Division of the Eastern Hockey League and then played Syracuse in the EHL championship. In the first game of the championship series, Horne scored three times, a hat trick.

Now, hat in hand, this all-star player was walking the streets of Macon, explaining the rules and selling advertising for the game program. The challenge of selling hockey was enormous, even for an all-star. Horne was especially pleased when C&S Bank devoted a full-page ad to explain the fourteen hockey penalty signs. The young model perfectly executing the hockey penalty signs was dressed in a football cheerleader's uniform, complete with a pleated skirt.

When the ad copy arrived, Horne knew his job had only begun.

A Face Only His Mama Could Love

Pen in hand, Tony McMichael studied the piece of paper he was about to bring to life. Let's see. A few more locks of hair here. A little five o'clock shadow there. Needs a little more biceps, don't you think? How about teeth? Better make 'em optional.

This certainly wasn't the most difficult assignment of McMichael's career as an illustrator and graphic artist. It was about the most intriguing, though. The new hockey team had commissioned him to design and create a mascot and a logo. The logo would be challenging enough—an emblem that would be recognizable throughout the league, at the top of the team's letterhead, and emblazoned across the chest of every player's uniform.

The mascot, however, would be the ultimate test. He must "invent" a Whoopee for the benefit of thousands of people who had no idea what a Whoopee actually was. Come to think of it, he wasn't so sure himself. But he was about to find out.

"I probably would have done it for free, just to get to do it," said McMichael. "It was such a fun idea."

McMichael had been working in the art department at *The Macon Telegraph* since graduating from the University of Georgia in 1970. He was a native son, of sorts, having grown up in Monticello, just 45 miles north of Macon, where he played football for Coach Bobby Holland's Monticello Hurricanes.

Admittedly, he couldn't even lace up his skates when it came to his knowledge of hockey.

"I didn't know much about it," he said. "I grew up playing football. I didn't even know they put on pads in hockey, so I was pretty ignorant of the sport. I had seen some games on TV, but I had never seen one in person."

He was pleased with his original idea for a logo—a rounded, capital "M" placed directly above a rounded capital "W," using the team's initials to portray a rounded hockey rink. To add to the clever emblem, the team sometimes joined the stacked "M" and "W" to form the double O's in Whoopees.

In giving birth to Mr. Whoopee, McMichael borrowed several characteristics from a mascot he earlier had featured in an advertisement for a local car dealership. Riverside Ford, a major sponsor of the team, had used McMichael's talents to come up with its "A. Giant." The "A" was for "Automotive," and the dealership used the caricature to hawk everything from Pintos to Mustangs.

John Shoemaker, the general sales manager at Riverside Ford, said the idea was to portray Mr. Whoopee as A. Giant's "first cousin from Canada." And there was a resemblance. But they were not twins.

"Mr. Whoopee was kind of a burly, French-Canadian," said Shoemaker. "He symbolized the players of that time. They were all down-to-earth and a lot of fun to be around. They were just good old country boys — from Canada."

McMichael was determined to give Mr. Whoopee his own identity and personality, and Buckley gave him the creative freedom to do it. The hockey team had only one request: Mr. Whoopee had to be twirling his index finger in the same fashion Johnny Carson did when he said "whoopee" on *The Tonight Show*.

Mr. Whoopee eventually took on many forms, and he truly was a work in progress. McMichael occasionally was asked to make minor changes. For example, in an early drawing, the mascot wasn't wearing the correct style of hockey skates.

McMichael would do several additional caricatures, including one for the cover of the game program where the mascot's arm was around KeKe. The team's pocket schedule showed a goal-tending Mr. Whoopee guarding the net while flashing a grin that displayed a missing tooth. In another drawing, Mr. Whoopee pulled off an opponent's sweater as the opposing player was flattened on the ice, lending new meaning to giving someone the shirt off your back.

"They gave me season tickets to the games. As I went to the games and learned more about hockey, I began to appreciate all of the little nuances about the sport," McMichael said. "I began to make Mr. Whoopee look more physical. I refined him as I went along. There just wasn't enough time. It all went rather quickly."

Yes, that did seem to be a problem.

So many caricatures, so little time.

Mr. Whoopee's
Northern Exposure

Kim Lander was minding his own business during a public ice skating session at the Coliseum when Wayne Horne came up and introduced himself. "Where did you learn to skate like that?" Horne asked him.

Lander was flattered. It's not every day that the No. 1 draft pick of the local hockey team pays a compliment to you on your skating prowess. But the 21-year-old Lander actually did carry some modest credentials to the floor of the Coliseum. He had been born in New Jersey before moving to Macon as a small child. He had an uncle, Don Tingley, who once played for the Toronto Maple Leafs. Lander might not have done any high sticking in his lifetime, but he was teaching a little high karate at the time.

Horne and Lander became friends. And it wasn't long before Lander was pounding the pavement with Horne to sell advertising for the Whoopees' program. Then Lander found himself assuming the duties of assistant team trainer for a team that was still months from completing its roster.

Soon, there was another assignment. "They needed somebody to drive the team van to training camp," he said.

No problem, Lander said. He was just thrilled to be working for a professional hockey organization. There was, however, one catch. As the puck flies, the training camp in North Bay, Ontario, was a straight shot due north. But there would be a slight detour to the northeast.

"We had to go get the equipment," said Lander.

Oh, well. New Haven, Connecticutt, was only 500 miles out of the way. So the journey began to take the shape of a sweeping curve. Lander and Horne were marked men when they pulled out of Macon. They were, after all, driving a Riverside Ford van with the Mr. Whoopee caricature painted on each side. You can't expect to travel incognito when you're cruising in something with Whoopees all over it. There were strange looks. There was finger-pointing. Lander looked out and could see those sharing the road with them laughing when they caught a glimpse of the van. Nothing like having your own traveling carnival at sixty miles per hour.

In New Jersey, he glanced over and saw a television crew filming the van as it rolled down the turnpike.

"That night, we were lying in bed in the motel room, and we saw ourselves on TV!" Lander said. "It was funny. We had no idea. There they were, in New Jersey, talking about the Macon Whoopees from Macon, Georgia."

But the curiosity was only beginning. After picking up the used equipment the Whoopees had purchased from the New Haven Blades hockey team, Lander and Horne turned their wheels toward North Bay.

At the border, Canadian officials took one glance at the odd-looking van and decided to do some investigating. "Just what the hell is a Macon Whoopee?" one guard asked.

Lander launched into his explanation for what seemed like the 1,817th time. The name. The song. The team.

"A hockey team?" said the guard. "In Macon, Georgia?"

The novelty did not subside once training camp opened in North Bay and workouts began at the Double Rinks Arena.

"It was as if the people already knew us before we got there," said Lander. "When they found out I was from Macon, they kept asking me if I knew the Allman Brothers."

There was a fascination with the team for several reasons. First, there was Mortson, a hockey legend around North Bay. After a journeyman playing career, this was KeKe's first crack at coaching—and he had brought his team home to Ontario for auditions.

"KeKe and hockey just went together," said Pete Handley, the sports editor of the *North Bay Nugget* newspaper. "He had been playing for so many years for so many teams and at so many levels that you were not surprised at anything he did in hockey."

Second, it had been a long time since professional hockey had a presence in North Bay. Both the Cleveland Barons and Chicago Blackhawks held training camps there in the 1950s and '60s, but it had been more than a decade since a pro team had trained in the area.

And then, there was the name. What's next? Eddie Cantor headlining a concert at Double Rinks?

"I think there was some disbelief that it was, in fact, a real team," said Bob Dupuis, one of a whopping nineteen goalies brought into training camp. "We went through our share of it for playing on a team with a name like that."

The atmosphere, though, was pretty special. That much was apparent. "It caused a big stir around town," said Dupuis, who made his home in North Bay. "The rink was full, and this was just training camp. All the local sports fraternity came out to see the team."

It didn't hurt to have a drawing card like Doug Harvey, either. The NHL Hall of Famer was director of player personnel for the Whoopees' parent club, the Houston Aeros, and stayed in training camp to help Mortson. The Whoopee wanna-bes were in awe of Harvey, who had played on five Stanley Cup championship teams for the Montreal Canadiens and who had won the James Norris Memorial Trophy for best defenseman in the NHL seven times.

"He was the Bobby Orr of his day," said Dupuis. "Every kid our age in Canada knew who Doug Harvey was."

Under Mortson, the training venue on the outskirts of town had been transformed into nothing short of boot camp. The team was up jogging every morning at 7 A.M. and on the ice from 8-10 A.M. After lunch, Camp KeKe resumed its two-a-days between the dasher boards from 2-4 P.M.

"Everything with KeKe was robust," said Al Rycroft. "He was a very high-tempo individual. He kind of knew who was going to be on the team, so he picked his favorites right away, and I happened to be one of them. We got to test all of the new players coming down, especially the goaltenders. Bob Dupuis was the one we really had to test because KeKe liked him but wanted to make sure he could withstand the pressures of the shooting gallery you had in that league."

Conditioning and making cuts weren't the only things on Mortson's agenda. In his own way, he was bringing his team along and forcing them to bond together.

"KeKe always made sure we had lunch and supper together," said Horne. "That was important to him. In the evenings, we would go shoot pool or go to a movie, but we all had an 11 P.M. curfew."

Training camp was not without its share of pranks and practical jokes. Rycroft unknowingly had heat rub poured in his underwear before one practice session. Another time, Mortson and Harvey accidentally hit a bird while driving to the rink. Instead of giving it a proper burial, they took it into the locker room and shoved it into team captain Ray Adduno's skate.

Trainer Roger Gibson also joined the team in training camp. He had come over from Espanola, about sixty miles west of North Bay, for an interview. Within minutes of meeting Mortson, Gibson, who had never been farther south than Dayton, Ohio, was ready to join him for a bowl of grits in a place called Macon, Georgia.

"I had never had an interview with anyone quite like him before," said Gibson. "He made me feel at home. He treated me like a son. I said I would go south with him."

So they left behind the nearby Georgian Bay for a place called Georgia. They left behind North Bay for a place where the only bay was a song written by Macon's own Otis Redding: *Sittin' on the dock of the bay, watching the tide roll away.*

They left behind birch trees and shadflies for magnolias and mosquitoes. They rolled out of town in a Whoopee van and an assortment of Galaxies, Impalas, Mustangs, and Pintos. They crossed through border towns, watched for all the speed traps, and set their compasses for the deep South. As the latitudes changed, so did the temperatures. The accents.

It was early October.

The leaves on the trees were beginning to change.

If only they had known how much their lives were about to change, too.

Don't Shoot Me, I'm Only the Hockey Player

Shoot! Shoot! Shoot!

Every hockey player hears those words as he rushes the net. Thousands of times. Millions of times.

But the Macon Whoopees probably never dreamed that "shooting" would be so closely identified with the law-and-order mayor of their newly adopted hometown.

Ronnie Thompson was his name, and "Machine Gun Ronnie" was his claim to fame. In the turbulent early '70s, he had made national headlines with his "shoot to kill" orders. Billboards around town were not of the "welcome wagon" variety. They were warning labels: "Beware: Armed Robbers Will Be Shot."

"I am encouraging the police to shoot anyone engaged in an armed robbery," he said in December, 1970. "I want them to shoot. We will ask questions later."

Thompson, who had no college degree, twice had been elected to the mayor's office. He was a man of many talents, and he once recorded a gospel album produced by soul singer James Brown. He was considering running for governor. (He later ran in the 1974 state primary as both a Republican and a Democrat.) And his tough-guy stance on crime had been lauded by national radio commentator, Paul Harvey.

And, oh yes, there was the tank. It definitely put Macon on the map—at home and abroad. Once, a local librarian, vacationing in France, picked up a copy of a Paris newspaper, and there, on the front page, was an international wire photograph of Thompson and his tank!

"That Ronnie Thompson was a legend," KeKe later would say. "He was ten times bigger than we ever were."

Thompson never really wanted to be called "Machine Gun," but he did nothing to discourage the image. No matter how many industries he recruited, hospitals he built, and roads he paved during his administration—all without the benefit of a bond issue—his reputation followed him like a hired gun.

Actually, he never even fired a machine gun. It was a .30 caliber police carbine. He fired it in a moment of self defense after a sniper shot at lawmen on a tense summer night at a local housing project in 1971. It was during the Fourth of July weekend, and Macon had been hit by scattered firebombings, robberies, and sniper incidents. Thompson responded by imposing a curfew and declaring a state of emergency. He took to the streets himself on a Saturday night, in a display of his own leadership, and grabbed the gun.

The morning newspaper spiced up the story claiming it was a Thompson brand—a manufacturer of "Tommy" sub-machine guns. "I called the reporter and asked him why he said I fired a machine gun when all I did was shoot a couple of rounds with a carbine," Thompson said. "He told me it was 'more colorful.' I personally didn't think it looked too good for the mayor to be out engaging in that kind of activity, but it was a spontaneous thing. I didn't go there to grab somebody's (gun) and start shooting."

Although he wasn't flattered with his initial portrayal, Thompson soon began to warm to this idea of a smoking gun legacy. A jeweler by trade, he began selling gold machine gun tie clasps. The first order of 1,000 was snapped up at $1 each. They were sold in all 50 states and New Zealand. Later, he marketed a T-shirt with the caricature of a duck firing a machine gun below the words: "Keep on Duckin'."

His machine gun antics were only one layer of the spit-fire mystique of Ronnie Thompson. He did, after all, buy the city a tank. That's right. A tank. Not a water tank or a fuel tank but a bam, bam, stick-'em-up 'mam, honest-to-goodness tank.

"An armored personnel carrier," said Thompson.

It could have been considered paranoia. It may have been called purely reactionary. But, as crime seemingly spiraled out of control in the city, Thompson wanted to protect the home front as the rest of the wicked world closed in on Macon.

America most definitely was not at peace with itself. During the same year that Thompson took office in 1968, both civil rights leader Martin Luther King Jr. and presidential candidate Robert F. Kennedy were killed by assassins' bullets. The span of the next three years would be equally turbulent.

At home, Macon, a town that had once had segregated rest rooms, was trying to adjust to federal court-ordered school integration. Anti-war demonstrations were popping up all over the country, including the deadly riot at Kent State. There were Black Panthers and an underground group called the "Weathermen." And Charles Manson emerged as one of America's most famous mass murderers.

The mayor became particularly concerned after an incident in New Orleans in which seven policemen were killed after a militant group opened fire from a hotel. After learning that national groups could be targeting policemen for assassination attempts, Thompson began searching for an armored personnel carrier. But the cost was too prohibitive. The tanks started at about $150,000 and usually cost about twice that amount.

But Thompson had been known for his ability to pull a few strings in Washington, and he soon had an armored personnel vehicle on its way from the Army's depot in the south Georgia town of Thomasville for only $200—the cost of shipping and handling. It was funded through the city's civil defense program, and Thompson would later name it the "Winky Tink" after civil defense director, W.H. "Wink" Dubose.

He had it delivered on a flatbed truck—in broad daylight—and it arrived at the transit authority's bus depot. After a few weeks, the drab, olive-colored tank had caused such a commotion that Thompson ordered it moved into a garage under lock and key. There, it was painted red, white, and blue.

It was large enough to carry twenty-five officers. Although there were reports the vehicle would be equipped with a .50 caliber machine gun and cannon, Thompson said it never had any weapons. "It was strictly for defense rescue operations," he said. "It even had rubber tires so it wouldn't mess up the streets."

Not even training camp could have prepared the Whoopees for Machine Gun Ronnie. He once sent the tank over to greet the team during a workout at the Coliseum. As a practical joke, several of the French-Canadian players were mock "arrested" for being foreigners. Some still had on their skates.

Said KeKe: "We thought it was for real when he wheeled out

that big tank. He 'arrested' my players and put them in the tank. It was all meant in fun, but a couple of players still had their skates on that day, and one of them said: 'I'm not getting on any tank.' And they (the policemen) pulled guns on 'em. Ronnie knew about it, and I knew about it, but the police they sent didn't know. They were from the riot squad or something."

Shortly after the team arrived in Macon, Thompson invited the players to ride on the tank. Using stepladders, the Whoopees and other team officials climbed aboard and hung on for a ride.

"We rode into town on that bloody tank," said Rycroft. "It was smoking, full of diesel fuel. I wasn't sure what to think. It was an event, all right. We didn't know who Ronnie Thompson was, but we found out he was a bit of a different sort of guy, with his own tank!"

"I remember the noise of it all and how unusual it was to be riding through the center of town on a tank," said Ron Morgan.

Gibson, the trainer, also was treated to his first tank ride. He had brothers who had served in the army and navy branches of the Canadian military, but he had never been in the armed forces.

"It seemed," he said, "like we were going to war."

Well, maybe not war, but at least to City Hall. People stopped on downtown sidewalks to watch the grand entrance of the team, even if it was on top of a tank. Thompson issued proclamations naming each of the Whoopees honorary citizens of Macon. A photograph was taken, one that was later used as a team Christmas card.

"I felt safe," said Horne. "No one was going to hurt us on that tank."

Not everybody, though, was rolling out the red carpet from Mulberry to Poplar Streets and down Cotton Avenue. "A lot of people must not have liked the team from the start," said Lander. "As we were riding through town, one lady came up and started shaking her fist."

"Why don't you go back where you came from?" she yelled.

The tank rolled along, with everyone aboard trying to ignore her.

After all, the Whoopees were invincible.

The whole thing *seemed* bullet-proof anyway.

Friday Night at the Fights

Although no one knew it at the time, or could even have anticipated it in their wildest dreams, a future President dropped the ceremonial first puck on opening night for the Macon Whoopees. Georgia Governor Jimmy Carter slipped and scooted to center ice and, with a flick of his wrist, slapped the inaugural puck of the Southern Hockey League onto the colossal ice cube on the Coliseum floor.

The league office sent a giant wreath in the shape of a horseshoe.

For good luck, of course.

It was 7:15 P.M. on Friday October 12, 1973. The rest of the league would be fifteen minutes behind the start of the Macon Whoopees and Suncoast Suns.

The cold war was about to begin.

"It was perfect," said Fierro, who was doing the public address system. "A Canadian game and a Manhattan accent all crammed into the Macon Coliseum with an opening night crowd of high school football and professional wrestling fans."

As the game got under way, Fierro made the announcement that President Nixon, in the middle of his Watergate scandal, had selected Gerald Ford as his vice president to replace Spiro Agnew who had resigned from office.

Carter, who would defeat Ford in the Presidential election three years later, had barely settled in his seat from dropping the puck when the fists were flying across the ice faster than you can say: *"Whooooopppppppeeeeeee."*

The opening night crowd of 3,000 fans gasped and blinked in disbelief. The game was less than a minute old when Whoopees' center Ray Adduno and Suncoast defenseman Blaine Rydman were trading knuckles as if they were the undercard to Ali-Frazier.

After the smoke had cleared and a little blood had been wiped from the ice, the two trouble-makers were sent to the penalty box

47

for five minutes for fighting. A second fight broke out just nine seconds later between Macon's Norm Cournoyer and Suncoast's Jacques Royer.

Slide over and make room in the penalty box. It was going to be a long night. The game was less than two minutes old, and it already had been delayed for 17 minutes because of the fighting.

"The ice was covered with equipment, and there were pockets of brawls all over the rink," said Ellis Pope, who was covering the game for the *Telegraph*. "You could actually see blood dripping from some of the noses and faces. And that might have been what doomed the Whoopees right there in their first home game. The fight lasted so long and was so entertaining that you soon heard fans saying: 'Aw, this stuff is fake. It's just like wrestling.' Many fans, who were more accustomed to seeing body slams and arm drags, actually thought the fights were staged."

Was this really what Pinkerton had in mind when he delivered his Patton-like preseason sermons? *"If they didn't keep score, they'd call it war."*

"I think that was their whole game plan from the start," said Bobby Pope, the sportscaster who was filming the Whoopees' debut for WMAZ-TV. "They talked for weeks before the season began about how that was going to be their approach. I was eating dinner with Pinkerton one night, and he kept talking about how it was going to be a brawl. They were going to fight, fight, fight."

For many of the Whoopees, fighting simply was a fundamental part of the hard-nosed style that their player/coach, KeKe Mortson, demanded.

Brian Tapp, a rookie, had gotten into a skirmish with teammates Cournoyer and Ron Morgan a few weeks earlier in training camp. That, in itself, might have helped convince Mortson that Tapp had the kind of temperament that would be required to wear a Whoopees' uniform.

"Do you think you can play in this league?" Mortson asked him.

"I said, yeah, and he then asked if I would be willing to go through the end of the rink for him," said Tapp. "When I said, yeah, again, he said to me, 'I like you.' And, from then on, I was always on KeKe's line."

So it should have come as no surprise that Tapp threw some of the earliest punches in the opening night slugfest.

"In those days — and it's still true — touching the other team's goalie is off limits," Tapp said. "One of the Suncoast players hit Bob Dupuis, and I hit him about six times before he knew he was in a fight. Later, when I was in the penalty box, KeKe skated over to me and said: 'Way to go, kid. Don't ever let them touch your goalie.'"

The fights, however, reached the point of being excessive, especially for an impressionable audience that knew little about what to expect from their first hockey experience.

Macon was assessed ninety minutes in penalties overall — about three times the average — and Buckley was not pleased with the two bloody brawls right out of the chute. They quickly seemed to validate the sport's reputation for violence.

"I was livid," he said. "I went to the locker room at one point and said: 'Listen guys, the worst thing we can do in this first game is to have fights. This is a football crowd. They're here to see hitting and speed. The last thing we need is to come across looking like wrestling.'

"But we had a brawl. It turned out that we had a player and Suncoast had a player that had been bitter enemies with different teams in another league the year before, so they carried it out with a vengeance. From a public relations standpoint, it was awful."

It also overshadowed the opening night heroics of right winger, Al Rycroft, who stepped onto the ice and into the history books after scoring the team's first goal. He later would score with just 54 seconds left in a ten-minute, sudden-death overtime to give the Whoopees a 5-4 win. The winning play was set up when Cournoyer stole a pass from Suncoast's Pete Ford along the right sideboards and dumped the puck to Rycroft who was in front of the Suns' goal.

"The pass from Cournoyer was perfect," said Rycroft. "Norm made a great steal and then passed to a perfect spot for me to shoot and score. It was like clockwork, just like we had practiced it.

"The goalie came at me, and I just let it fire. It was a big night for me. It was the first winning goal for a first-year team. To score the first goal and then the winning goal—especially in overtime—that will always be special."

Not everyone was there to eyewitness it, though.

"We played the second period and came back for the third, and nobody was there," said Rycoft. "Almost everybody had gone home. They thought it was like a basketball game with a first and second half."

Macon's Aubrey Allen, attending his first hockey game, thought it was over long before that. "I walked down to the locker room at the end of the first period to congratulate them for playing a good game," said Allen. "That's when they told me the game wasn't over yet."

All those months of trying to educate the public about hockey—and even holding an open house and rules demonstration on the eve of the first game—apparently had not put enough emphasis on teaching the rookie fans how long to stick around for the game. After all, hockey games are divided into three parts.

Said Buckley: "A lot of people who were there had to wake up the next morning and read in the newpaper that there was a third period."

Still, there was a sense of pride from most everyone in the Macon organization. The maiden voyage now was under way.

"I was proud and happy about the job we had done getting Macon ready for hockey," said Horne. "I really was convinced on opening night that hockey was a hit."

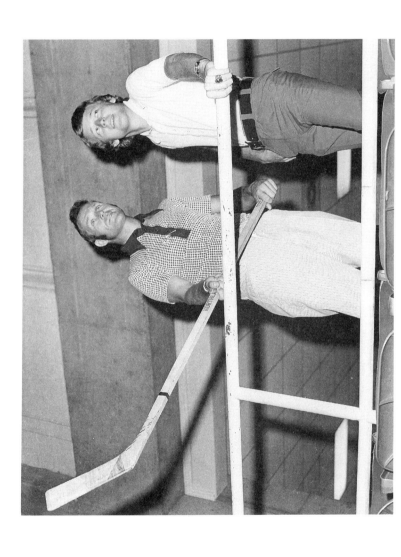

1. July 4, 1973 at the Macon Coliseum was a day of "firsts." It was KeKe Mortson's first head coaching position and Bill Buckley's first job out of college. (Photo courtesy of *The Macon Telegraph*)

2. Top Salesman and Top Promoter: Whoopee owner Jerry Pinkerton and Coliseum Manager Bill Lavery. All they needed was money—lots of money. (Photo courtesy of *The Macon Telegraph*)

3. Sittin' On the Deck of the Tank: This snapshot, taken on top of Mayor Ronnie Thompson's tank, would later be used for a team Christmas card. (Photo courtesy of Bob Dupuis)

4. "We rode into town on that bloody tank," said Whoopee Al Rycroft. "I wasn't sure what to think. It was an event all right." (Photo courtesy of *The Macon Telegraph*)

5. The Whoopees had their own float in Macon's holiday parade. Their name was misspelled on the left side of the float, just another example of the hockey team's identity crisis in the Georgia city. (Photo courtesy of *The Macon Telegraph*)

6. Opening Night, October 12, 1973: After 90 minutes of penalties, mostly for misconduct, many fans left the game thinking they had been to a fight where a hockey game broke out. (Photo courtesy of *The Macon Telegraph*)

7. Jerry Pinkerton, Bill Buckley and Macon Mayor Ronnie Thompson at center ice for opening night festivities. The league office sent the team a floral horseshoe for "good luck." (Photo courtesy of *The Macon Telegraph*)

8. Would it work? The local newspaper, *The Macon Telegraph,* wrote: "Trying to sell ice hockey in the South is like trying to unload surfboards on Eskimos." (Photo courtesy of *The Macon Telegraph*)

Playing Diehard to Get

There were many things Dan Jaskula wasn't going to miss about living in Chicago. But he dearly missed hockey.

After moving to the Middle Georgia area in 1972, he began having withdrawal pains. It wasn't easy going from Blackhawks to Cold Turkey. It was killing him. With no local hockey team to follow, winter would be one big sinus headache.

That changed when he returned from a trip and went to pick up his cats at his mother-in-law's house. He had missed the big news. The Whoopees were in the delivery room.

"Guess you're going to get your wish after all," she told him.

He's not exactly sure when the excitement wore off, or if it ever did, but the next morning he was on the phone to Chicago. He called his good friend, Wally Phillips, who was in the middle of a popular morning radio show on WGN.

"A hockey team? Are you going to have ice down there?" asked Phillips, trying to get in some long-distance ribbing.

"It's kind of hard to play without it," Jaskula shot back. "But you're probably never going to guess what they named the team."

"No, I probably wouldn't," Phillips said.

"The Macon Whoopees," said Jaskula.

There was dead air in the Windy City.

"OK, what's the joke?" said Phillips, breaking the pause.

Jaskula was thrilled. It wasn't long before he found himself bonding with other diehard hockey transplants who had crossed the Mason-Dixon Line on a power play.

"I talked about hockey until I was blue in the face," said Jack Billman. "I had been the timekeeper for the Cincinnati Mohawks before moving to Macon in 1967. I was hoping like. the dickens that people would accept the sport here. I felt that if we could just get them to come out and watch, it would get them interested."

Jaskula went a step farther. He promoted. He educated. Like the Whoopees front office had done in the weeks and months before, Professor Jaskula began enrolling unsuspecting friends in his own version of Hockey 101.

"About a month into the season, we had a 'This Is Hockey' program at the Exchange Club in Warner Robins," Jaskula said. "We went through the basics. This is a puck. This is a net. It was very elementary. We did a lot of schooling."

When it came to hockey, Bill Ashmore admittedly ranked among the illiterate. He never had been to a game, and barely had even watched the game on television until he attended the Whoopees game on opening night. He still doesn't know exactly what lured him there, just that he's glad he went.

"I guess it might have been the novelty of it," he said. "A hockey team in Macon? It would be kind of like having a ski jump team in Macon. You might go just to see how they were going to do it."

Since Ashmore had some rough edges around the fine points, he had to take a crash course in hockey. He attended the first few meetings of the booster club. That was enough qualification to be elected president. Soon, he was planning events and collecting membership dues. He socialized with the players and invited many of them into his home.

"I was just an old country boy from the South," he said. "I had never been around French-Canadians. I didn't understand much of what they were saying, but they couldn't understand me, either."

In hockey vernacular, Ashmore soon was guilty of hooking. He invited Alan and Geri Frank to a game.

"We knew he would be disappointed if we didn't go," said Geri Frank. "I never had been a sports fan in my entire life. I was the kind of person who went on a date to a football game and took a book of poetry with me. So I got dragged to this hockey game. My first impression was that these people were beating up each other. It was terrible. Then I really started getting into it. I remember saying to myself: 'Oh, there's a dark side to you, Geri.' We never stopped going after that. During the season, a bunch of us would pile into the car and go to places like Charlotte to watch the Whoopees on the road."

It wasn't long before Macon had captured converts and cultivated diehards. Though often small in number, the loyalists behind the Whoopees turned up the volume.

"They never stopped cheering from the moment you stepped onto the ice. It was vibrant," said Al Rycroft. "If you couldn't play for a crowd like that, you couldn't play hockey."

It was a curious blend of young and old, Yankee and Rebel, male and female, white collar and blue collar.

"It was an event," said Bill Elder, a local disc jockey. "Macon didn't have that many new things. You could go to church, go to Arby's, and then go to the Whoopees' game.

"The younger people always seem to be more willing to experience a new sport than older people," Elder said. "There was a faction that was there to see the fights. They really didn't care who won the game. It was a step up from wrestling. You didn't have to feel guilty about being there. It was kind of like watching lions in tuxedos."

Sisters Ima Jean and Thelma Tharpe were among the most vocal fans in the building every night, taking their seats in section 108 and ringing their cow bells until the cows came home.

"We got close to several of the players, especially Georges Gendron," said Ima Jean Tharpe. "My sister helped him do his income tax. Georges used to tell her she reminded him of his mother. She laughed and said she didn't want to be his mother. She wanted to be his girlfriend! When his mother did come down to visit in January, she and Thelma could have passed for twins."

Carson Flournoy was among those who, once they started attending the games, had a hard time staying away.

"It was fun. It was different. It was infectious," he said.

"I had never been to a hockey game until the Whoopees came to Macon," said booster club member, Larry Younis. Once he made that first trip to the Coliseum, he was hooked.

"I loved it," said Younis. "I remember somebody told me you couldn't enjoy hockey unless you were there in person. I found out that was true. TV just couldn't do it justice. When I went, I realized that there's stuff going on everywhere. You just can't see it all on television."

Bob Maurus, made trips from Atlanta to Macon with his sister, Lauri, to watch his future brother-in-law (Bob Dupuis) play goalie for the Whoopees.

"We would stop at the Krystal for a couple of sliders (hamburgers) on the way to the games," said Maurus. "You didn't have to eat those suckers, just tilt your head back and let 'em slide."

Maurus admitted being a hippie who liked hockey. "That was back during the days when there were hippies and rednecks," said Maurus. "That time of the '70s was the meeting and merging of these two groups. You worked with each other and realized that the hippies were decent guys and so were the rednecks."

One of the many places the hippies and rednecks found themselves sitting next to each other was at the Macon Coliseum for a hockey game.

"The great thing about Macon was it was minor league and all the fans could get close to the action," said Maurus. "Before making the trips with Lauri down to see Macon play, I had watched a few games on television. Hockey just always seemed to me to be one of those sports that is impossible to watch on television. You miss all the ballet out on the wings."

Rabid fans were in short supply, though. Soon, the numbers began to catch up.

"It got lonely," said Johnny Jones, who rarely missed a game. "There was a nucleus of people that you would see at every game. But most of the time, there weren't a lot of other folks there."

Empty? Bobby Pope was there every night filming for WMAZ-TV. Those thousands of fans were disguised as empty seats.

"On some nights, you could have shot a cannon through there," Pope said.

"It was very hard trying to get it off the ground," said another fan, John Minnich. "It was so empty in the Coliseum that you could hear all of KeKe's locker-room language from the stands."

And then there was Leroy. Leroy didn't have to say much.

Leroy lived in south Macon down the street from the mechanic who worked on Brian Tapp's used Corvette. Leroy was big enough to block out the sun.

"I asked my mechanic about him one day because I had to drive by him every time I went to the shop," Tapp said.

"Are you afraid of him?" asked the mechanic.

"He's the biggest man I've ever seen in my life," said Tapp. "He was always lifting weights and must have weighed about 350 pounds."

The mechanic told Tapp that Leroy often came with him to the hockey games. "He loves you because you're always getting into a scrap," said the mechanic.

That night, in a game against Roanoke, Tapp looked up during warm-ups and spotted Leroy. He skated over to SuperFan. "If you're ever at a game and you see that I'm on the bottom, feel free to help out," Tapp told him.

Tapp didn't disappoint Leroy nor, as it turned out, did Leroy disappoint Tapp. Tapp got into a "scrap" with Roanoke defenseman Serge Beaudoin. They both ended up in the penalty box, and they were still going after each other when the rather large Leroy walked down and stood over Beaudoin.

"Sit down and shut up," he told Beaudoin.

A bit stunned, Beaudoin looked over at Tapp.

Said Tapp: "Don't mess with me while my fans are around."

Strike Up the Band, and Everything Else

Bob Barnette was stirring a bowl of tomato basil soup as the memory of the song stirred in his head. He didn't seem to care that he was sitting in a crowded downtown restaurant. He began to hum. Loudly.

Another bride, another June. Another sunny honeymoon. Another season, another reason. For makin' whoopee.

A lot of shoes, a lot of rice. The groom is nervous, he answers twice. It's really killin', that he's so willin', to make whoopee.

It was an old refrain from an old song. He picked up his soup spoon as if it were a baton, and he was ready to lead the Central High School pep band—one more time—through another rendition of the Gus Kahn song.

"When they contacted me and told me the name of the team, I wrote an arrangement of 'Makin' Whoopee'," said Barnette. "It wasn't the kind of song you would expect from a sports team. It was not a fight song. It was a love song.

"But it *was* unique."

So was the idea of a high school band at a minor-league hockey game. Thirty members of the Central band, along with the school's drill team, showed up for every home game and filled the Coliseum with an array of tunes and dance numbers.

They played "Makin' Whoopee" during warm-ups. And they played it every time the home team slapped pucks past goalies from places like Charlotte and Roanoke.

Another season, another reason ....

"Needless to say, about 99.9 percent of our kids had never been exposed to hockey," Barnette said. "We enjoyed it because of the contact we had with the players. And they loved us. Of course, the team was all male, and I had a drill team of about forty girls. That didn't hurt.

"One Saturday, the team invited the band down to the Coliseum. They put us all in skates and gave us each a hockey stick. I tried it and fell all over the place. I body-checked myself several times."

Barnette decided to return the hospitality by inviting the Whoopees to a Central home football game at Porter Stadium. The players met the band and drill team at the school to ride over to the stadium on the bus. "About a dozen of them showed up right on time with sports coats and their hair combed," said Barnette. "They all came up to shake my hand, grinning from ear to ear. That's when I noticed for the first time that almost none of them had teeth. They *all* needed some bridgework!"

Not even a pep band could pep up the attendance, though. After the initial novelty of having a hockey team in Macon began to wear off, the players and the band both found themselves playing in front of sparse crowds. That's when two Macon girls — Talisa (Thompson) Hanson and Suzanne (Bullard) Markert — decided that the Coliseum crowd needed more than saxophones and a tuba section. What the franchise needed was some rah-rah team spirit, so they appointed themselves as Whoopee cheerleaders.

Of course, they had to get permission first.

They were, after all, only twelve and thirteen years old.

"We loved ice skating, and we went to a lot of the games," said Hanson. "We decided the reason not many fans were there was because they needed some cheerleaders."

With Buckley's approval, the girls were given a designated spot in one of the end zones where they could lead the fans in cheers. They put up posters along the railing, occasionally brought their megaphones, and, of course, shook their pom-poms for breakaways and power plays.

"We would holler and scream and do our 'Whoo, Whoo, Whoopee' cheer," Hanson said. "When we still weren't getting enough crowd participation, we thought it might be because we were so little, and we needed to be more visible. We asked Mr. Buckley if we could sit on top of the penalty box."

"No way," said Buckley.

It was a big deal being *the* cheerleaders for the Whoopees. Although the two girls were cheerleaders at Miller Middle School, they were most proud of their unique designation at the hockey games.

"We told *everybody* at school," said Markert. "We took it on as our own adventure. After the Whoopees gave us the OK, we went for it. We did it for free, but it was almost like being hired for something. We had the official approval. It wasn't like we were out there screaming on our own."

They made a lot of noise. Sometimes you could hear their tiny yells in the cavernous Coliseum. Sometimes the *Whoo, Whoo, Whoopee!!!* was swallowed by other sounds..

"We felt like we were the little sisters to all those fellows out there," said Markert. "It was kind of like fighting for the underdog."

Chief Big Stick

There were no blue lines out on Lake Nipissing, and only a few rules. This rink stretched as far as Mike Penasse's eyes could squint, but not as far as his dreams could take him. On the banks of the Ojibway Indian Reservation near North Bay, Ontario, he honed his hockey skills using rocks for pucks and small branches for hockey sticks.

"As soon as the ice froze every winter, we were on that lake from morning until night," Penasse said. "We barely took time out to eat. It was take a bite and back you go."

Tina, one of his seven sisters, taught him how to skate. He was thirteen years old before he went with a friend to an indoor rink in nearby Sturgeon Falls for a tryout. He was too shy to venture onto the ice.

"There were all these French-Canadian guys around," he said. "I didn't know what I should do. It was the first real rink I had been on. Somebody pushed me out there. I don't know who it was."

It wasn't exactly a miracle on ice, but it was a start. It wasn't long before Penasse had forged a reputation as one of the area's top young players. "All of the skills I had learned from pond hockey and road hockey seemed to carry over," he said.

Within five years, he had been drafted by the Houston Aeros of the World Hockey Association and assigned to Macon. When he arrived, they immediately began calling him "Chief." The nickname stuck.

"We pictured him on horseback and living in a teepee," said Buckley.

That was hardly the case, but it was only part of the mystique of Mike Penasse. Things weren't quite that primitive in his native community of Garden Village where there were few paved roads and even fewer electric appliances.

"He was the first in our family to go away," said his mother, Rita Penasse. "I didn't think he would stay. He grew up in this community, and I gave him one or two months. I thought he would get homesick."

Penasse went through training camp with the Aeros and introduced himself to the legendary Gordie Howe by greeting him with a body check. In return, Penasse got a stick slap on the back by Howe. "It still hurts," Penasse said, laughing.

If Houston taught him anything, it was that he was indeed a *long* way from the reservation. His jaw dropped enough to accommodate a couple of pucks when the Aeros traveled to New York City for an exhibition game.

"It blew my mind," he said. "I had never seen people on the street like that, not even on TV!"

At eighteen, he wasn't quite ready for prime time, so Houston shipped him to the Whoopees to play for Mortson. KeKe was familiar with the Indian. Mortson's home in North Bay shared an opposite shore on Lake Nipissing.

"I've got a kid who may turn out to be the best player in the league," Mortson would tell people. "You just wait and see!"

Maybe it was his flair, the way he skated, or the way he handled the stick. Or maybe it was the idea of having a hockey version of the Atlanta Braves' Chief Noc-a-Homa slapping a puck around the Macon Coliseum that was so appealing.

From the opening face-off, Penasse established himself as one of Macon's most popular players. Females were attracted to his rugged good looks. The Central High pep band, greeted him with an Indian drum beat when he took the ice. And, for those fans looking for blood and guts, Penasse was not afraid to put up a good fight. That wasn't totally his nature when he arrived in Macon. But Mortson vowed to toughen him, to find that mean streak, and have it streak down the ice.

"We would be on the way home from a road trip, and KeKe would be up in the front of the bus having his beers. He would call me up there and start getting on my case about not being able to fight," Penasse said. "There were ten guys on the team bigger than I was, and I was the one doing all the fighting. I don't know why."

Mortson got his wish. At 5-foot-11, 175 pounds, Penasse eventually would lead the Whoopees in penalty minutes. In one game, he carried his fight into the penalty box and tried to scale the partition to get in a few more licks at his opponent.

If Penasse never could get a clear idea of his role with the Whoopees, at least he left Macon with a clearer view of the world. He started wearing contact lenses.

Cliff Corley, a local optician, had been asked to fit several of the players with the soft contact lenses that had just become available on the market. Hockey is one sport that doesn't recommend eyeglasses, for obvious reasons.

Penasse was one of Corley's patients, but his case was unique from the others. Penasse was far-sighted, and he was prescribed to wear "plus" lenses, which were still being test-marketed.

Corley called the director of research at Bausch & Lomb and received permission to use Penasse as a case study.

"Although I fitted several other players with contacts, Mike was the key to the whole research," Corley said. "Minus lenses were readily available, but I had to get Mike's lenses through research and development. I had to pay more attention to him because of the study."

Corley would regularly attend the team's practices to check on Penasse's progress with the contacts. He also befriended the young Indian, inviting him to his home to spend time with his family. "He was young, couldn't speak English clearly, and he was a little scared," Corley said.

A slight challenge presented itself during Corley's research. At first, Penasse could not manage to insert the lenses by himself. Corley spent hours trying to teach him the procedure. On road trips, goalie Bob Dupuis had to put Penasse's contacts in for him.

"I called Bausch & Lomb and told them we were having a difficult time," Corley said. "The guy said: 'You've got to teach him. That's part of the study. If you can't, we can't use him. Offer him anything! Take him to get a steak and send me the bill!'"

One day, Corley kept Penasse in his office and told Dupuis to leave. He didn't want the Chief to have to rely on his back-up.

"Mike kept saying: 'Bob, please don't go,' but I told him that if he would learn to do it today, I would take him out and buy him a steak dinner," said Corley. "He had them in his eyes in ten minutes. I thought to myself: I should have done this a month ago."

Mortson, for one, was grateful.

"KeKe would tease me," said Corley. "He would say: 'You've got to make that boy see better.'"

So he did.

A new sport was born in Macon. Just call it eyes hockey.

Soft Ice and a Hard Sell

He took the entire team to Florida, just as he said he would. They would play the Suncoast Suns in the Sunshine State. KeKe was a man of his word.

In Macon, the Whoopees had split their first two games of the season with the Suns. The schedule then carried them to "God's Waiting Room" for a two-game series with Suncoast in St. Petersburg. Many of the French-Canadian players never had seen palm trees and white sandy beaches — except in travel brochures.

"I promised them that they all would get to see what Florida looks like," Mortson said.

But reality soon would catch them by the tailpipe. There were twenty-two players on an eighteen-man roster. In hockey, slashing is supposed to be against the rules, except when you occupy the seat of general manager. Then it becomes a way of life.

KeKe Mortson, the born optimist, had been at the receiving end of hundreds of stitches in his hockey career. For a man who didn't mind open wounds, he sure dreaded another kind of cut.

"The hardest part of hockey is telling a guy he has to go," said KeKe. "If a guy was a rat, it would be easy. A lot of people don't know what it's like to wake up at 4 A.M. and lie there for two hours trying to think of a way to tell a player he is no longer on the team."

Just as Governor Jimmy Carter had been the special guest of the Whoopees on opening night, Lieutenant Governor Lester Maddox got into the Whoopee act when the team returned to Macon on October 24. Maddox, the former governor and a longtime national political figure in his own right, was presented with a Whoopees T-shirt.

"He immediately put it on," said Ellis Pope. "I'll never forget the picture. Here was a guy who had been governor of the state wearing a Whoopees T-shirt and a pair of shoes that hadn't been shined since the day they came out of the box."

The season was only three weeks old when Pinkerton began to

groan. In a game against Greensboro, only 900 fans walked through the Coliseum turnstiles. Said Pinkerton: "We have to do something to get more fans in the stands." He wasn't about to push the panic button, but his finger was poised.

When the Whoopees hosted league-leading Roanoke two weeks later, the game was delayed 20 minutes while officials waited for the ice to re-freeze. The explanation was a power failure in a cooling unit that caused a portion of the ice to melt. Pinkerton, however, knew better.

"Lavery (the Coliseum manager) said to me: 'Roanoke's coming in here, and they're pretty fast. Let's soften the ice,'" Pinkerton said. "That night, there was slush water flying everywhere. So KeKe said to Lavery: 'Turn it down a little more. I think we've got them.'"

Macon won that night, 8-1, and the team hovered around .500 for the first month of the season. But the early part of November exacted a toll as the team lost six of eight games. The ice began to harden around Mortson, too. He accused himself of being too soft on the players. No more Mr. Slush Guy, he vowed.

"I was trying to be a good guy to the players—a buddy, a father. But from now on I'm going to run this team the way I know how," he said. "With discipline. And I mean strong discipline."

No matter how hard the Whoopees tried, more cracks were beginning to surface. The team waived two of its marquee names—veteran Blake Ball and first-round pick Wayne Horne. It was six weeks into the season, and the Whoopees were averaging just 1,800 fans per game, about only half of the attendance standard of 3,500 set by the league. It was obvious the team wasn't making much whoopee at the box office.

"I looked at the books every day," said Buckley. "I saw how much money we spent, and then I looked at how much money was coming back in, and it was ridiculous."

It was not a scare tactic. Buckley said the team would rather give away tickets than to try to threaten its fragile relationship with a fan base still trying to learn about the game. He promised the franchise would not just pick up and leave, as had happened in some cities.

"We're trying to be honest with the people of Macon and Middle Georgia," he said.

The team did pick up the pace and began to play well, moving into second place. But it became even more obvious what hockey was up against while trying to gain a foothold in football country.

The Whoopees' home game against Charlotte on November 21 had to be rescheduled so it wouldn't fall during the same week as the big Central-Warner Robins high school football playoff game.

A home game against Greensboro in early December was billed as a chance to see a "Jackie Robinson" on ice skates. Alton White of the Generals was the only black player in the SHL. He had been farmed out to Greensboro from the Los Angeles Sharks of the World Hockey Association, where he was the only black player in that league, too. White also held another distinction. In seven years as a pro, he never had been involved in a fight on the ice. The irony was not lost on anyone as the December cold moved in.

Not a fighter?

The Whoopees were beginning to realize that, if they were going to survive, they would have to fight for their lives.

"We're not at all like the rest of Georgia. We have a saying: If you go to Atlanta, the first question people ask you is, 'What's your business?' In Macon they ask, 'Where do you go to church?' In Augusta they ask your grandmother's maiden name. But in Savannah the first question people ask you is 'What would you like to drink?'

— *From* Midnight in the Garden of Good and Evil

Praise the Lord and Pass the Puck

There are references in the Bible to victory and defeat, cheering, endurance, goals, courage, bruises, choking, revenge, sticks, fighting—and even ice. In the Baptist hymnal, there are titles that would make good hockey fight songs—"Nothing But the Blood," "A Mighty Fortress," "Victory Must Be Won," and "Blest Be the Tie That Binds."

But nowhere can one unwritten rule be found. If there was an 11th Commandment, it most surely would be:

Thou shalt not schedule hockey games on Wednesday and Sunday nights.

Welcome to the Bible-thumping South, where you don't cross-check the routine of attending church functions at mid-week and on the Sabbath. With the delayed start of getting the team organized—Macon was the sixth and final franchise added to the SHL for the inaugural 1973-74 season—the Whoopees didn't have much choice. The Whoopees weren't being baptized. They were being dunked.

"We just ended up with those dates because, at the league meeting, we were the new team," said Lavery, the Coliseum manager. "Coming in, we should have expected we were going to get the worst dates. There were only so many Fridays and Saturdays, and we had to go back and take what we could get."

Tuesday and Thursday nights were reserved for professional wrestling. To try to bump wrasslin' from its traditional weeknight perch would have been sacrilegious. But there was no panic. Actually, the Whoopees' front office didn't seem to mind the schedule at first glance. Fierro took a look at the schedule and saw the nine Sunday home dates—more than any other day—and eight Wednesday night contests and couldn't believe the Whoopees' good fortune. And, because Pinkerton was a Yankee, he understood Fierro's enthusiasm for Wednesday and Sunday hockey.

"I remember telling Jerry that Wednesdays and Sundays were like a dream come true," said Fierro. "Wednesday and Sunday are the days that hockey has been played in this country for years. In New York, New Haven, Pittsburgh, Hershey...everywhere."

Everywhere except the South.

"Who knew that those were the nights people went to church? There were no Protestants in the North, at least not *that* kind of Protestant," said Fierro. "Macon was a good hockey town. You have to have a town that has an undercurrent of blood-lust in it as best expressed by professional wrestling. The only problem was that even the wrestlers were in church on Wednesday and Sunday nights!"

Nowhere was this more evident than during the first two months of the season when the Whoopees were averaging about 2,000 per game. The least productive night was Sunday when the average attendance was barely over 1,000 fans. Wednesday didn't fare much better with about 1,300 fans.

It was tough for KeKe, Al, Brian, and the Chief to compete with Matthew, Mark, Luke, and John.

"They automatically were cutting out a huge percentage of people," said Steve Johnson, who was the associate pastor at Mabel White Memorial Baptist Church, one of the largest congregations in the city. "By scheduling games on Wednesdays and Sundays, they were starting off by excluding a large number of people in a very religious community.

"The church is a major hub for social interaction. In those days, the Little Leagues would never schedule games or practices on Wednesdays or Sundays. They knew the kids weren't going to come. They were going to be in church."

Georgia's 108-year-old Sunday "blue laws" were typical of Southerner's attitudes about anything that didn't have to do with hymn singing on the Sabbath. The state's blue laws, sometimes known as "closing laws," made it illegal for a citizen "to pursue his business or work of his ordinary calling on the Lord's Day."

Of course, not everything was considered sacred. Lauri Maurus, who was dating goalie, Bob Dupuis (and later married him) remembered getting ready to go to one Sunday night game with her brother. Given the team's track record on Sundays, there would be plenty of good parking and seats available. There was no real need to hurry to the Coliseum. "The schedule in the newspaper said they were going to play their usual home game on Sunday," she said.

Imagine her surprise when she approached the Coliseum and found a line of headlights was wrapped around the building. "The parking lot was packed, and there were all these trucks," she said. "People were swarming in and dressed differently. We went to 'will call' to pick up our tickets, and there were all these people. I remember thinking to myself: 'Finally, people are going to support the team.' We were in the lobby, and, all of a sudden, we heard this Vroom! Vrooom!"

She knew it wasn't the Zamboni, the giant machine that smoothes the ice. The schedule in the newspaper that morning had been wrong. The Whoopees weren't playing at home. Lauri found herself at a tractor pull.

Amen.

Headlocks and Body Slams

In the office next to his at the Macon Coliseum, Buckley heard Choo Choo Lynn's booming voice. "Hey, Whoopees. You in there?"

Choo Choo Lynn was the local wrestling promoter. He knew everything about wrestling. He knew Mr. Wrestling No. 2 without his mask and could tell stories about the night Andre the Giant tried to take on half of the Coliseum crowd.

"If you think your sport is going to knock my game out of Macon, you can pack up now," said Lynn. "If you want to see how to put people in a building, meet me here tonight. I'll show you a crowd."

Nice to meet you, too, Buckley thought to himself.

That night, Buckley was still in his office making phone calls when Lynn appeared in the doorway. Buckley was *going* to see wrestling in Macon. "The place was packed," said Buckley. "They were all screaming and yelling at the wrestlers. One little old lady — she must have been 80 years old — left her ringside seat and was at the edge of the ring shaking her cane at one of the wrestlers."

As they stood and watched, Choo Choo smiled at the pure, unadulterated passion the fans had for his sport.

"They love it. They live for it," Choo Choo said. "There are people in here that spent money to buy tickets instead of paying their rent. Your problem is nobody knows anything about '*iiiice hockey*.' You gotta make 'em love something they don't know anything about. Wrasslin' is in their blood around here. It's part of who they are."

When he said it, Choo Choo made "*iiiice hockey*" sound like malaria. In spite of all the arrogance, Buckley knew Choo Choo was right. If the Whoopees were going to do well, the people had to love it. And to love it, the Whoopees had to get the locals to try it. How could hockey get to be as popular as wrestling?

Buckley had a sociology degree. Three months earlier, he had been writing term papers on crime and punishment, the history of race relations, and the cultural effects of the Vietnam War. He didn't remember a text chapter on how to get wrestling fans excited about ice hockey. The only thing Buckley had going for him was his memories of attending the Generals hockey games in Greensboro.

"I remember when it was stick night or some other give-away night, I had to get my dad there early," said Buckley.

Drawing from that memory alone, Buckley and the Whoopees went after the kids like the Pied Piper. First, they held a hockey clinic. Horne and Mortson provided skates, sticks, and pucks to children. The idea was to teach the youngsters about hockey. Get them to love it. Then, they would come and bring their parents — and then everybody would love hockey. The turnout was light. It was youth football season, and everyone was at practice. Youth football almost killed the Whoopees. When they announced that all of the players could get into the Whoopees' games for free, Buckley had no idea the parents would simply drop off the kids at the door. His dad had *never* done that.

The Whoopees later announced that young football players would be admitted free with a paying adult. The story in the newspaper said, "Whoopees officials feel it will be safer for the youngsters." Certainly it would be safer for the Whoopees' bank account.

The drive to get young people, and their ticket-buying, money-spending parents involved in hockey took an unusual spin in early September. Pinkerton announced that he had signed the first female hockey player in the Southern Hockey League.

"Patty Lynch is coming to Macon," beamed Pinkerton. "She will help us promote hockey in general with special emphasis on junior hockey."

At age twenty-five, Patty was a flight attendant for Eastern Airlines when the airline decided to form a hockey team in Atlanta. Because she had played hockey in Michigan since she was eight years old, Patty became the only woman on the roster. There was instant fame. After being featured by the Atlanta media, Patty was interviewed by *Sports Illustrated* and the *London Observer*. She stumped the panel on "What's My Line" and appeared in hot pants on *The Tonight Show* teaching Johnny Carson how to hold a hockey stick and shoot at a goal.

Now Pinkerton had added "Patty" under "Doris" on his Macon dance card. "I'm really excited about coming to Macon," Lynch told the *Telegraph* from her Atlanta home. "It's great to teach ice hockey, especially in a town with a team named the Whoopees."

Pinkerton had grand plans to draw the kids. He announced an idea to form a little league that would play prior to Whoopees games and between periods. He also wanted a group of all-stars who would travel to play the best youth from other SHL cities. Pinkerton wanted local businessmen to sponsor teams and provide uniforms and equipment for the league.

"Patty will also form the first girls team in the South," Pinkerton said. "We will call the team the 'Dixie Cats'."

But Patty never played a down in Whoopee-town. It was all a publicity stunt.

While Eddie Cantor's "Makin' Whoopee" was spinning at 45 rpm's, Pinkerton was spinning out of control. And the ideas just "kept on comin'."

"I had all of these public relations folks with all kinds of promotional ideas calling on me," said Buckley. "One of the first questions they asked was: 'What's your promotional budget for the season?' Not only did we not have a budget—I had to sell the Volkswagen I drove to Macon just to open our bank account."

Then there was stick night. The Whoopees gave away promotional hockey sticks to the first 500 kids. There was T-shirt night. The first 300 fans got free T-shirts at the door.

When it came to competing against football, the Whoopees knew their best approach was "join 'em...you can't beat 'em." While Gene Brodie's Central High football team, which called itself the "Big Orange," was enjoying an undefeated season, the Whoopees had "Big Orange" night. When football season ended, the Whoopees started their Sunday games in the afternoon—but not until the NFL season was over.

There was Noonday Optimist Night, when the local civic club bought tickets for 250 kids. There was Armstrong Cork Night and Ladies Night, when all of the ladies got a free ticket.

Fan Appreciation Night was scheduled for a Wednesday. The first 100 kids were to receive a free puck with the Southern Hockey League logo. It was church night. It was a school night.

There were pucks left over.

Pinkerton promoted a night for the local newspaper and the radio and television stations to buy blocks of tickets for employees and advertisers. In announcing a special Civic Club Night and a ticket deal, a Whoopee spokesman sounded desperate saying, "They can bring *anybody* they want."

"What we should have had was a Baptist night and a Methodist night. That might have worked," said Buckley. "We should have had a deal where you went to church on Wednesday or Sunday night and then came to the Coliseum for the second and third periods—for two-thirds of the cost of the ticket."

That way, churchgoers could have shouted "kill 'em" shortly after saying the benediction.

The Whoopees also figured that the few fans who did come to the games needed to have fun so they would come back.

"After the first period of the first game, there was a bloody yo-yo tournament that took forever," said Al Rycroft. "It took an hour to get the tournament finished so we could start the second period."

There were broom hockey games between civic clubs, lucky seat drawings, and another refrain of "Makin' Whoopee" by the Central High Band.

"One night we had a 'shoot-the-goalie' contest, and a guy was shooting at this plywood cutout of 'Mr. Whoopee' standing in front of the goal," said Pinkerton. "There was a hole cut in Mr. Whoopee's stick, and if the shot went in, the guy won a car— which I would have had to pay for."

When the puck left the young man's stick, it looked dead in the hole. "I remember looking up and saying, 'Please, Lord, make that hole smaller,'" said Pinkerton. The shot missed. Pinkerton's prayer had been answered.

The Whoopees program ran a crowd photo each game of a fan from the previous game. The photo of the individual was circled with the caption, "Did you get caught makin' whoopee?" The winner collected two free tickets to the next game.

Still, the promotions were failing to put seats in the seats. So Pinkerton floated "rumors" that Doris Day was coming to Macon to sing "Makin' Whoopee" and that the Allman Brothers were going to record the song.

The Whoopees' front office was criticized by the local media for the "sideshow" between periods. They were encouraged to "try to sell hockey as hockey." Nowadays, the game features skating mascots, concerts between periods, and Zambonis that appear to be wearing Halloween costumes.

Kind of makes a marching band and a yo-yo contest look tame.

Empty Seats, Empty Pockets

"I can't even skate. My legs go in every direction."
— *Whoopees' owner, Jerry Pinkerton.*

Leave? Why, they couldn't do that. They just got here.

Yet Macon had barely been dusted with its first frost of the season before the talk began. You know, the old argument about irreconcilable differences. Oh, Pinkerton had talked about the possibility of pulling up skates. But seriously, folks, the MACON Whoopees wouldn't work any place besides Macon. Would they?

"All I said was if (the fans) don't like it, you can't force it down their throats," Pinkerton said. "You just move the franchise. Then, the next morning's headlines said: 'Whoopees May Move.' I said: 'Oh, gosh!' A guy from Warner Robins called me and said: 'Jerry, you're not leaving, are you? We've got season tickets.' And I told him I didn't say that!"

By Pearl Harbor Day, Pinkerton had publicly pledged that the Whoopees were staying put and clarified that he had no intention of moving the team. He said Macon's fans were terrific. There just needed to be a lot more of them. Said Buckley: "What we need is to convert our faithful following of 1,000 into 5,000."

Pinkerton began working to reorganize the team's financial structure. Of course, it didn't help that the Whoopees boasted the highest payroll in the league. It also didn't help that the wolves were lining up at the door. Ship and Shore, a local travel agency, had filed suit against the Macon hockey team in Bibb Superior Court for debts of $2,720.48.

Euthanasia had begun. As they battled their own set of financial problems, the Whoopees watched the Suncoast franchise go belly up in mid-December, less than halfway through the season. There would be no more trips to Florida, no matter what KeKe promised. The SHL was down to five teams.

It wasn't easy being optimistic when there was too much

74

month at the end of the money. The Whoopees' first check in December came bouncing back like a rubber puck. They had become members of a new league—the NSF (Not Sufficient Funds).

KeKe's wife, Clara, told Buckley that KeKe wasn't sleeping well at night. It showed. He looked tired and irritable. By late December, with his team battling a slump of losing seven out of eight games, Mortson announced he would resign after Macon's game with Charlotte on December 30.

First the Checkers, then checkmate.

"(Pinkerton) owes me $18,000," said Mortson. "He owes the team a month's salary. How can you coach in a situation like that? It appeared we had unlimited funds, but now no one is getting paid. These (players) have to worry about their families."

As the last hours of 1973 ticked away, the Whoopees turned to the league for help. Pinkerton went to the SHL's board of governors meeting in Charlotte and asked that the team's $25,000 franchise fee be returned in the form of an emergency loan.

Pinkerton hoped not only to borrow money but to buy time as he sought potential investors in a limited partnership. The league said: 'No, thanks.'

Instead of quitting, Pinkerton returned to Macon with empty pockets and a steadfast promise. "I'm not going to run out on the club or the city," he said. "I don't want people to think that I'm a thief. I'm confident we will get back on our feet."

Mortson was convinced to remain with the club, and the players rallied behind their popular player/coach. The front office begged the fans for patience. On the first day of the New Year, the day typically reserved for resolutions, the Whoopees toughened their resolve. "As long as there is ice, we'll be on it," Buckley promised. "And, if the ice melts, we'll buy water skis and play on the water."

But there were tell-tale signs of going under in the days and weeks ahead. The debts had reached about $150,000, and the team bounced its second payroll in as many months. KeKe walked into Buckley's office where Buckley was adding up the latest bills.

"Where's Pinky?" he asked.

"I don't know, KeKe, probably in Atlanta," Buckley said.

"Well, what's he doing there and where's the money?"

KeKe walked out of the office, down to the locker room, and said he was going for a skate. An hour later, he was back in Buckley's office.

"Billy, we need to talk. Let's go for coffee, eh?"

They walked to Mortson's Torino in silence. KeKe was the first to break it.

"You OK, Billy? You look bad."

"Yeah, I'm OK," Buckley said. "Let's just go some place where nobody knows who we are."

They sat down over coffee and eggs.

"Billy, what do you know about this organization?" KeKe asked.

Buckley said he thought it wasn't really Pinkerton's team, that someone else was financing the club—the millionaire from Atlanta, Tedd Munchak. Buckley said he thought that since Munchak already owned the team in Greensboro, Pinkerton was his front man, allowing him to own two teams in the league without breaking the rules.

"Billy, I was told we had a million-dollar hockey team," KeKe said. "That's why we went out and got some of the best players we could find. Pinky told me money was no problem."

Buckley spoke up again. This so-called corporation was a flop. There were no books, no money other than what the team took in from advertisements and ticket sales, which wasn't much. He told KeKe there was little chance the team could meet its next payroll. He said the Whoopees were on the verge of facing public embarrassment of more lawsuits from local businesses. The team owed one local sporting goods company about $13,000. There never had been a budget. It had been an incredible snow job on the credit system.

Buckley then told Mortson he was going to quit. Enough sixteen-hour days. Enough bouncing paychecks, irate phone calls and having to hoodwink the players on payday. It just wasn't worth it. KeKe then made a saving shot.

"Billy, this is the greatest experience you'll ever have," he said. "I'm the one who ought to give it up. I'm the one with a family who is losing a year of income. I'm the one who ought to quit. You've got everything in front of you, everything to learn. Don't quit, Billy. Whatever happens here, you'll be a better person for it."

Just What Size Do You Wear, Tricky Dick?

Richard Nixon will be remembered for many things. His foreign policy. His "Checkers" speech. His "I am not a crook" speech. And a little scandal known as Watergate.

Pinkerton wanted him to be known for something else. So he sent him some Whoopees T-shirts. Nixon, of course, wasn't the first celebrity to be the recipient of a white, 100-percent cotton piece of Whoopee. Johnny Carson once held one up on *The Tonight Show*. Actor Paul Newman had become the first on his block to own one.

"I gave away hundreds of those T-shirts," said Pinkerton. "They were like gold."

Still, Pinkerton wanted Nixon, the most powerful man on the planet, to have a Macon Whoopees shirt in his wardrobe. If Nixon could gain fame for framing his fingers in the "V is for Victory" sign, then surely Mr. Whoopee's twirling index finger couldn't be far behind in the chief executive's repertoire.

So Pinkerton sent some T-shirts to 1600 Pennsylvania Ave., and waited for the obligatory thank-you. Nixon, of course, was in the middle of a nationwide fuel crisis and under the gun over Watergate. The thank-you note must have slipped his mind. The Whoopees had a few problems of their own. The ice beneath their feet was melting into a sea of red ink. Nevertheless, Pinkerton did wonder if Nixon was going to acknowledge receiving the shirts.

"You know, I don't know why Nixon never wrote me back after I sent him those T-shirts," Pinkerton said. "I decided to call him. I called the White House and said I'd like to talk to President Nixon.

"The first person who answered was Mrs. Barbara Armstrong. She asked who was calling, and I said it was Jerry Pinkerton from the Macon Whoopees and that I wanted to talk to the President. She said: 'Oh, those T-shirts! We had so much fun with those T-shirts!' She then put me through to Rosemary Woods. Mrs.

Woods said: 'Jerry, the President would like to talk to you, but he's busy. I'll tell him to call you.' I said to have him call me anytime."

Pinkerton eventually got a letter from Nixon postmarked January 16, 1974, thanking him for the shirts. The Whoopees moniker had to bring a smile to Nixon's face. After all, his wife, Pat, had a small part as an extra in the 1936 musical "The Great Ziegfield," which won three Academy Awards, including "Best Picture," and included the "Makin' Whoopee" tune on its soundtrack.

The Nixon letter was a bright spot during a week when the Whoopees were on the verge of folding. The mounting financial difficulties had forced Pinkerton to try to raise as much as $175,000 from investors to ensure that the club would remain in operation for the rest of the season.

"*Sports Illustrated* wanted to know if Nixon ever called me," said Pinkerton. "And I said he may have tried, but business has been so bad around here they cut off my telephone."

Ifs, Ands, and Butts

Brian Tapp stepped onto the ice for practice wearing nothing but his skates and a hockey stick. As he made a few naked laps around the rink, his teammates realized what had happened. They had just been "streaked." "Streaking" was happening during political meetings, football games, and picnics.

There was a lot of "streaking" taking place on college campuses. A girl, wearing nothing but a smile, would "streak" through a boys' dormitory. Or fig leaf-less guys would "streak" past a sorority house.

It's only appropriate to consult *Webster's Collegiate Dictionary* for the definition: "To run naked through a public place." It wasn't a crime. It was good clean fun. And that's the naked truth.

Tapp, who had lived in the collegiate world for three years prior to giving hockey a try, obviously had enrolled in "Streaking 101."

"I went for a little skate," Tapp said. "After about two or three minutes, I went to go off the ice, and KeKe said 'No, you're here, like this, for the two-hour practice.' And the guys started faking shooting pucks at me.

"No, I didn't fall down," said Tapp. "But it did get a little cold out there after a couple of hours. I never streaked again."

Well, not exactly. Because elephants can't skate and John Deere doesn't make Zambonis, the Coliseum ice had to go when the circus and those infamous tractor pulls came to town. That left the Whoopees all dressed up with no place to skate. As a result, Mortson called Pinkerton who arranged for "ice time" at a suburban Atlanta ice rink. For the players, going to practice now was a road trip.

While "streaking" had its moments, "mooning" was another popular activity at the time. *Webster*, again (just so you know we're not making this up): "To expose one's naked buttocks."

"We were on the way to practice in Atlanta, and I was riding with Roger Gibson and a couple of the guys in the Whoopee van," said Tapp. "We were going through Atlanta, and we caught up with KeKe in his car.

"I was sitting next to Roger in the front, and, as we passed KeKe, I told him to go by slowly and honk," Tapp said. "So, we go by—and I moon him."

Now, get the picture. Mortson looks to his left to see a van with a cartoon guy twirling his finger through the air—and "naked buttocks" hanging from the passenger side window. No face...just buttocks. Without a name.

"We had a great laugh all the way to the rink," said Tapp. "When we got to practice, KeKe immediately told everyone to pull down their pants."

The coach slowly examined each derriere looking for clues. He was determined to get to the bottom of this.

"Tapp, that's $200," said Mortson.

"How did you know it was me?" asked Tapp.

Said Mortson: "Because of the mole on your cheek."

Everybody laughed. Tapp should have realized everyone remembered the "naked two-hour skate-a-thon."

"I didn't mind the moon, but you're in the official Macon Whoopee equipment van. I just won't take that," said Mortson.

So, did he really collect the money from Tapp?

"Oh, yeah. He charged me in front of all the guys," Tapp said. "Then, about a week later, he called me over and gave the money back to me."

Norm Metcalfe was the designated driver of the official Whoopee car. In addition to the van, Riverside Ford had loaned the Whoopees a new four-door LTD. "I always ended up with a carload of guys when we practiced in Atlanta," he said.

On one of the return trips from Atlanta, after a tough morning practice, Metcalfe, Dupuis, and several other Whoopees pulled up to a red light.

"Everybody was still numb from practice," said Metcalfe. "I was staring out the windshield, waiting for the light to change."

And then it happened. "I heard one of the back windows go down," said Metcalfe. "I turned around, and Dupuis had stuck his butt out the window. His 'cheeks' were holding an unlit cigarette."

At the intersection, next to the car full of whoopee, an unsuspecting motorist sat with his window rolled down. The guy turned to look.

"Hey, buddy," Dupuis said in a deep voice, "got a light?"

"I remember thinking: 'Now that's a goalie for you,'" said Metcalfe. "Everyone was just howling. I said: 'Bobby, he just saw your best side.' We had a lot of fun. It seemed like each day brought more jokes, more laughs."

There were smiles all around. And certainly no thoughts that, one day, there might be a dark side of the moon.

"I don't own the clothes I'm wearing. And the road goes on forever."

– *The Allman Brothers,* Midnight Rider

The Road Goes on Forever

They never issued him a uniform number or had him suit up for a game. But whenever the Whoopees were on the road, he might as well have been on the team roster.

Now playing bus driver, B.C. Musick.

With a name like Musick, it somehow was appropriate that he drove the bus for a team that coined its nickname from a song.

"They treated me like I was one of the players," he said. "They would even let me sit on the bench with them. KeKe would say: 'Come on over and sit with us. We don't want you to get into any trouble.'"

Trouble? Well, there had been a few times when Musick was known to get a bit vocal. Once, after driving the Columbus College basketball team to a game in Savannah, he had become so incensed with a referee's call while sitting near the Columbus bench that he was whistled for a technical foul.

But that was basketball. This was hockey.

Was there a special penalty box for bus drivers?

Musick, two minutes for high lipping.

KeKe would occupy the front seat. He constantly would chatter and puff on his cigar.

"I really didn't know anything about hockey," Musick said. "But I learned a lot from KeKe. Sometimes, he would take me to the side and show me how to do this and that. He gave me a copy of the rules."

The players called him "Bussie." Although he never played right wing for the Whoopees, he somewhat looked the part. When he was nine years old, another child had pushed him from behind, chipping his front tooth. Later, after two tours of duty in Vietnam, the military doctors had ground it down so much it finally broke off.

The road had pretty much been a way of life for Bussie. As a driver for Trailways, he had been transferred to Macon and had driven charters for several Capricorn Records recording artists, including The Allman Brothers Band and Wet Willie. He also briefly drove for James Brown's band.

He had taken senior citizens on trips to Canada and high school students on senior trips to Florida. He had transported Little League all-star teams to Kentucky, Boy Scout troops to New Mexico, and the Warner Robins High football squad on Friday nights to hostile stadiums in places like Valdosta and LaGrange.

"I once drove the Allman Brothers tour bus for 22 days. I tell you, it was a lot different hauling a rock band around," he said. "I never felt as close to them as I did to the hockey team. Whenever I took a band on the road, I would just go to my room when we got to the motel. When I traveled with the hockey team, the players always would invite me out to eat with them or to go to a movie. You treated them right, and they treated you right. It was like family."

The Southern Hockey League schedule was equally divided between thirty-five home dates and thirty-five road games. The pace was demanding with seventy dates crammed into twenty-two weeks, giving the Macon team an average of 3.1 games per week.

There were times when the Whoopees were a bigger draw on the road than they were at home. Maybe it was the intriguing nickname. Maybe it was the colorful coach. Maybe it was both. Said one Greensboro fan: "With Macon and Mortson around, it's a shame the Whoopees don't get a percentage of the road gate. I'll keep coming just to see them play."

Connecting the mile markers between the SHL venues in such towns as Roanoke, Charlotte, and (before the Suns folded) St. Petersburg took time, patience, and a good sense of humor. Some players would sleep on the bus. Others would play cards. Plenty of jokes were passed up and down the aisle, along with some of the tallest tales this side of Winston-Salem.

"After the games, they would have me stop at a convenience

store," Musick said. "They each would come out with two six packs of beer and two quarts of tomato juice."

On road trips, the bus did not run on diesel alone. There always was plenty of Budweiser. The road was not without its share of adventures and misadventures. Once, on a trip to St. Petersburg, the ice became so soft during a game a fog developed over the surface of the rink.

"They had to stop the game and get the players to skate in a circle to circulate it off," said Gibson, the trainer. Suncoast might not have had many fans in the stands, but at least the Suns had a giant human fan on the ice.

On one road trip, the Whoopees were accompanied by Doug Harvey, the former NHL star who had helped KeKe in training camp. On the way to a game one night, the players were in their seats on the bus. Everyone was focused on the game, when, all of a sudden and out of the blue, they heard a plane fly close overhead. Suddenly, the nose of a DC-3 was overtaking the bus.

"We realized we were in the flight path for an airfield," said Dupuis. "We were getting close to where the road came to a 'T,' and the plane started to hit the ground. It was just the most god-awful landing you've ever seen. Bang. Bang."

Harvey, who was sitting next to KeKe, stood up and turned around.

"OK," he announced, "if you guys lose tonight, that's the plane we're taking home!"

George, Georgette, and Georgia

It was about 10 A.M. when Georgette Gendron settled into her seat.

She had just boarded a bus in her hometown of Sturgeon Falls, Ontario.

She had set a record at the bus depot. No one ever had purchased a ticket from Sturgeon Falls to Macon, Georgia. Although it took a while to figure it out, the fare was around $40.

It was January, 1974. Georgette was on a Mom mission. "I wanted to see Georges," Mrs. Gendron said with a sparkle in her eyes. "I wanted badly to see him play."

Georgette Gendron was her son's biggest fan. From the time he first learned to skate and hold his first stick, she was there. Getting him to practice. Getting him to games. All that Mom stuff. She had her memories, all right.

"I remember how beautifully he could skate," said Mrs. Gendron. "And how quickly he could start and stop."

She remembers watching Georges play hundreds of hockey games in rinks all over Ontario. "We would bring in empty tomato cans, fill them with nails, and shake them to make noise," said Mrs. Gendron. "We traveled to a lot of games."

But she never had traveled this far to watch Georges play. Her husband could not make the trip. She was alone. "I was squashed between passengers," Mrs. Gendron said. "I never had been to the United States, and I wanted to see everything. The bus stopped in every small town. I saw a lot of poor people, especially when we got to the South and Georgia."

After Toronto was in the rear-view mirror, the Greyhound rolled into the U.S. Detroit. Cincinnati. Knoxville. The seats were poorly padded and uncomfortable. There was no restroom. "I saw the sunset and sunrise from the same bus," said Mrs. Gendron. "When I left Sturgeon, I was wearing winter clothes. As we drove along and got more and more south, I had to peel off a few things here and there."

It wasn't easy to endure the long trip from north Ontario to south Georgia, but Mrs. Gendron had another motivation. She might not admit it, but "seeing Georges play" was not the main reason.

"I wanted to meet his new girlfriend, Gwin," admitted Mom. "When Georges mentioned marriage, I had to go."

Georges and the Whoopees were out of town on a road trip when the Sturgeon Express pulled into Macon. So Gwin met her boyfriend's mother at the bus station.

Of Gwin, Mrs. Gendron said: "She was pretty and well-educated. I liked her immediately."

Of Mrs. Gendron, Gwin said: "I was scared to death."

Oddly enough, Georgette Gendron was not the only Canadian parent visiting the Whoopees. Mike "Chief" Penasse's father, George, also had traveled from the Garden Village Indian reservation, not far from Sturgeon Falls, to watch his son play. He, too, was coming to America for the first time.

Although he took the bus, George Penasse could have hiked to Macon. He was a professional outdoorsman who spent his time trapping and hunting. He was a guide who could take people into the "bush" (wilderness) and help them hunt or fish. This was a talent he had learned as a long-time member of the Ojibway Tribe.

Penasse took his father on a sight-seeing tour of Macon. They played golf with some of Mike's teammates, and KeKe let Mr. Penasse travel with the team on a road trip.

"Mike and his dad talked on the phone a lot when Mike got to Macon," said Rita Penasse, Mike's mother. "George wasn't much of a talker, but one day he finished talking with Mike and suddenly just said, 'I've decided I am going to go.' I think Mike was really asking him to come."

George Penasse couldn't read. Without the ability to read maps and road signs, there was cause for concern. It was a long trip with lots of turns, right and wrong.

"I was worried about him," said Mrs. Penasse. "I thought he was going to get lost. If he were in the bush, he would be able to feel the wind and tell where he came from."

As soon as Mr. Penasse stepped off the bus, Mike took him to a local men's shop to buy a new suit to wear to the games.

Enjoying their sons' company, Mrs. Gendron and Mr. Penasse toured Macon, tested local cuisine, and met the other Whoopees players and fans.

"I know he had a really good time," said Rita Penasse of her husband's adventure. "I have a picture of him playing golf."

Mrs. Gendron and Mr. Penasse sat together to watch their sons play a home game in Macon. Georges gave his mother something he was good at—a goal. Mike gave his dad something he was good at—a penalty. Two minutes, elbowing.

While sitting in the stands at the Macon Coliseum, they even had their picture taken for the newspaper.

The longest road trip the two Whoopees players could remember was Macon to Roanoke. "I hated that trip," Georges said. "It was about eight hours on the bus to play a hockey game."

That's nothing. George Penasse and Georgette Gendron rode for twenty-two hours just to *watch* a hockey game. "I still can't believe they went through all that just to see us play," said Georges.

It obviously meant a great deal to have their parents in Macon to experience a game or two of their first professional season. It meant so much, in fact, neither would allow his parent to re-board the bus for the return trip home.

"Georges and I couldn't stand the idea of having them ride that bus back to Canada, so we came up with an alternate plan," said Penasse.

The plan? Two, one-way plane tickets home.

9. The original No. 99 was KeKe Mortson, not Wayne Gretsky. "KeKe went to Macon because he felt he could still play," said former Mortson teammate, coach and Detroit Red Wing great, Bill Dineen. "He gave the game 100 percent—more than 99 percent of all of the hockey players that ever played the game." (Photo courtesy of *The Macon Telegraph*)

10. Mortson looks on as Jim McMasters checks Roanoke's Claude Piche during a home game in Macon. (Photo courtesy of *The Macon Telegraph*)

11. The "signing" of female hockey player, Patty Lynch, proved to be nothing more than a publicity stunt. She appeared on "The Tonight Show" with Johnny Carson. She was a "no show" in a Macon uniform. (Photo courtesy of Dan Jaskula)

12. Buckley was proud of his new skates, a gift from KeKe. Later, KeKe gave him the rest of the uniform and a seat on the bench—not in the stands. (Photo courtesy of *The Macon Telegraph*)

13. Icing? Checking? Face-off? Macon fans had to take a crash course in hockey at almost every game. (Photo courtesy of *The Macon Telegraph*)

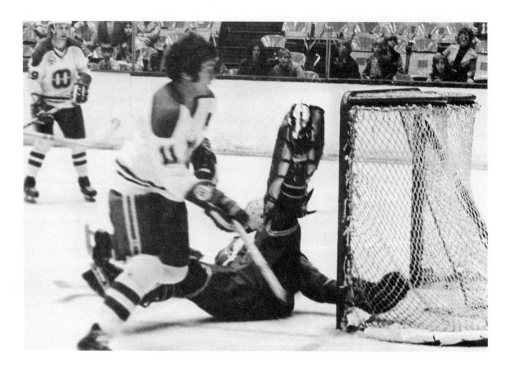

14. Al Rycroft (11) made history by recording the first-ever goal for Macon. "To score the first goal, and then the winning goal (in overtime) will always be special to me," said Rycroft. (Photo courtesy of *The Macon Telegraph*)

15. "We were hockey players," said goalie Bob Dupuis (30). "We weren't the smartest. I think it was when the third check bounced that we started to figure it out." (Photo courtesy of *The Macon Telegraph*)

16. Norm Metcalfe (16) faces off with Charlotte while Jean Fauteux (20), Mike Penasse (15) and 57 empty seats look on. (Photo courtesy of *The Macon Telegraph*)

17. Don Giesebrecht (14) scrambles to clear the puck to a waiting Norm Metcalfe. (Photo courtesy of *The Macon Telegraph*)

18. KeKe Mortson in action against Roanoke After scoring a hat trick against the league-leading Rebels, KeKe said, "I wanted to call a few of those guys who said I couldn't play any more and have a word or two. Couldn't do it though. The phones were dead." (Photo courtesy of *The Macon Telegraph*)

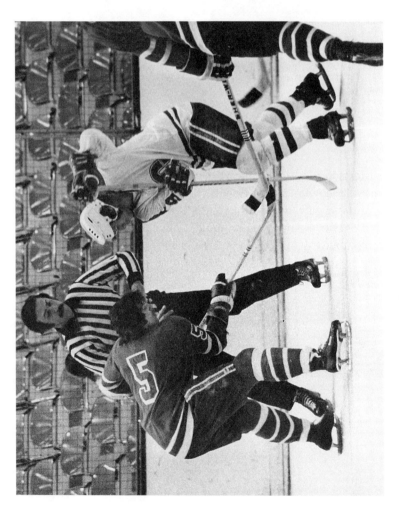

19. KeKe's outstanding play is witnessed by another "partial" sellout. (Photo courtesy of *The Macon Telegraph*)

20. After riding a bus from Canada to Macon, Georgette Gendron and George Penasse watch sons Georges and Mike play for the Whoopees. (Photo courtesy of *The Macon Telegraph*)

21. Buckley warms up for his 60 seconds of fame. After watching him skate in warm-ups, Brian Tapp turned to Buckley and said: "I'm glad we're not paying you to play." (Photo by Danny Gilleland, *The Macon Telegraph*)

Another Bride, Another Groom

Gwin Price was sitting on the floor of the Phi Mu Sorority house at Mercer University waiting for some whoopee.

"It was a Monday night, and we were having a chapter meeting. Some of the players were coming to the meeting to help promote the new hockey team," she said.

It was November 12, 1973, and the Whoopees' season was one month old. After starting the season with a blistering 4-1 record, the team had just returned from a 9-3 road loss to Greensboro. The record had dropped to 5-8-1.

Gwin didn't know Macon had a hockey team until she heard about the meeting from her sorority sisters. The Coliseum was located less than five miles from the Mercer campus, and the publicity in the local newspapers about the team had been unprecedented. How in the world could a college student not be aware of the new team in town?

"You really have to understand that Mercer was its own little community," said Gwin. "You didn't have a clue what was going on in the outside world. It was like a glass bubble."

Gwin either was on campus or with friends at Sean's, the unofficial Mercer hangout. Listening to the music of brothers— Allman and Doobie—Gwin and her sisters spent free time with each other after class, after studying, after sorority meetings— after just about everything.

Sean's had the basic elements needed for collegiate survival—a little food and a lot of beer.

The Price family was deeply involved in education. Gwin was one of three siblings attending Mercer in 1973. Her mother was a professor who had once taught Joe Namath in speech class while getting her masters degree at the University of Alabama.

Gwin's favorite activity was rolling with the Tide. "I was a Bear Bryant/Alabama/Joe Willie fan. That's all that mattered in life," said Gwin. "I learned about football because, in the South, the only time a girl was allowed to cross into 'guy territory' was to watch football.

"To communicate with the guys, you had to know football. I loved it then, and I still love it," she said.

With her sorority sisters, Gwin watched as Georges Gendron and three of his Whoopees teammates—Bob Dupuis, Gary Williamson and Mike Penasse—walked through the door for the chapter meeting.

"The players talked about hockey, trying to explain some of the rules and how the game was played," Gwin said. "They had equipment and uniforms with them, and they dressed to show us all the stuff they had to wear. Then, they picked a gorgeous girl in the room and dressed her up in the hockey equipment. When they finished, they told us they had free tickets for us to go to a game Wednesday night. That was great for us because we had 'Wonderful Wednesday' back then at Mercer, which meant that we didn't have classes."

So, like the rest of Macon, did they go to church?

"Of course," Gwin said. "We went to Sean's. That was church."

Although the Wednesday night hockey game was to be Gwin's first "live" visit to a rink, she was not a complete stranger to the game.

While in prep school in Massachusetts, Gwin was introduced to hockey. She fell in love with the Boston Bruins—Phil Esposito, Bobby Orr, and John McKenzie.

"I loved McKenzie," she said. "He was scrappy. He fought all the time."

Although she never made it to the Garden, Boston's games were broadcast on statewide television. She watched them with her friends in the dormitory. She was hooked.

"It was rough like football," said Gwin. "I liked the brutal force of it all. You could get animalistic and tell 'em to 'kill.' And, it was OK to do that. You could sit there and yell 'Get him! Hit 'em!' It's OK to yell that at a hockey game, just like it's OK to yell that at a football game."

On Wednesday night, all the Phi Mus attended the hockey game together. "Actually, we were late getting to the game," said Gwin. "On that particular Wednesday night, our sorority had a party, and we didn't get to the Coliseum until after the game had started. It was extremely fast-paced. I liked it more than ever.

"I loved the hitting and how physical the game was. It was really rough and a lot different than it appeared on television. I was impressed with the skill that was required to skate and pass the puck. Passing that puck and putting it exactly where it needed to be to score—that was fascinating."

After the game, the players invited the sorority girls to a nightclub known as The Butcher Shop. That's where Gwin spoke to Georges (Gendron) for the first time. At least she tried to talk with Gendron.

Problem: Southern girl meets French-Canadian hockey player and attempts to have meaningful conversation.

"Georges didn't speak English," said Gwin. "So, I don't even know how we got hooked up or how we even started talking."

Obviously, Gwin and Georges didn't really "talk" a lot. Dupuis had to be called in as an interpreter. Although it was Dupuis who deserves the credit for making the French connection, Janice Hunter played a major role. Janice was one of Gwin's sorority sisters and—more importantly—was her ride back to Mercer. Janice managed to leave Gwin that night with no ride back to campus. "Georges offered to take me back," said Gwin. "And, even though I barely knew him, I let him take me. That sounds terrible now. I would never let my children do something like that. But it was different back in 1973."

So, Wednesday, November 14, 1973, became Wonderful, Whoopee Wednesday. It was the night Gwin and Georges met and at least attempted to talk for the first time.

The language barrier challenge continued. The next day, broken English and all, Georges called Gwin to let her know that he was leaving her tickets for the Thursday night game with Charlotte.

"His English was so bad that it was hard to tell what he was saying," she said.

She did understand "tickets" and "will call window" and figured out the rest. She went. It was the first official date.

It was a great night for the Whoopees, too. Macon won 7-5 in a game that featured two shorthanded goals for the Whoopees. Gwin, of course, had her own fixation on this night.

Her best view of Georges came in the second period when Gendron again was sent to the penalty box for what was rapidly becoming his favorite infraction — charging.

The Gendron-Price relationship moved along in tenths. What Gwin refers to as "The Kiss" took place on December 10. "You know how you were always told that bells would ring — honest to God, it happened," Gwin admitted. "And we both said at the time of The Kiss: 'Oh my God, this is it!' I went and told my mother, 'This is it,' and she told me, 'No, Gwin, this is not it.' It was funny. All those years my mother had told me that 'I would know,' and now she was telling me that I didn't know. But, I did know."

Said Georges: "Well, it's just like you knew right away: 'What hit me?' She got hit at the same time and like, well, this is different — a different feeling totally. And you knew it instantly."

Leave it to a romantic hockey player to get "hit" by The Kiss. Some things don't change. Gwin's mother told her: "You are not marrying someone who doesn't speak English. He's a foreigner, and he doesn't have a college degree. He could get deported at any time."

This had to be tough on Dr. Gerri Price. Education was her life. This was the mother who was so focused on education that she sent her daughter to a prep school to prepare her for the academic rigors at Mercer. And now, with just one kiss, a French Canadian named Georges Gendron was the only subject her daughter seemed to be studying.

The relationship continued to move along in tenths.

On January 10, Georges asked, "Will you?" Gwin answered "Yes" and, a week later, Georges traded one of his Whoopees paychecks for an engagement ring.

On. Feb. 10, nothing happened, ending the couple's hat trick of tenths.

Four days later, on what should have been the happiest Valentine's Day for Gwin-soon-to-be-Gendron, fate finally hit the post.

Black Lines and Blue Lines

Vernon Colbert was skating when skating wasn't cool. He had taught himself to skate three years before the Whoopees were just a gleam in Jerry Pinkerton's eye. Unlike many of the Macon fans who curiously watched this slippery sport called hockey, Colbert at least could claim familiarity with the giant slab of ice on the Coliseum floor.

"When they started public skating at the Coliseum, I was anxious to see what it was all about," he said. "So I went down and rented a pair of skates the first day."

He always had been an athlete. He had played football in college and later refereed college football and basketball games all over the South. As a child growing up in Macon in the 1920s, he had bought a pair of roller skates. They were his first set of wheels.

"We used to get on the hill, skate down Calhoun Street, jump off the sidewalk onto Oglethorpe, and cross the trolley tracks," he said. "That's how we had our fun."

He knew ice skating would be fun, too, yet different. It would be trickier. Sure, he would use the same set of muscles and the same range of motion, but there would be no block of wheels for stability, just a long sharp blade.

At the ripe old age of 56, he knew this much, too. The older you are, the harder you fall.

Oh, it was shaky at first, almost scary. But he learned to stand, then negotiate his walk and glide as if the skates were merely extensions of his feet. Admittedly, he wasn't exactly doing figure-eights out there. Phil Esposito he was not.

"First thing I learned was not to be stupid," he said. "As you get older, the experience of falling and getting hurt makes you learn to take your time and work your way into it."

He was no expert nor did he profess to be. But, because he was at the Coliseum almost every night that the public skating sessions were available, he at least looked the part of someone who knew what he was doing. He hadn't just fallen off the back of a Zamboni, you know. Soon, he began teaching hundreds of children to skate using what he called "child psychology."

"Sit down and lace up your skates tight," he would tell them. "Now give me one skate, and I'm going to twist your ankle. Don't you let me twist it. OK, got that? Stand up. One thing you have to do is talk to your skates. What you have to tell your skates is: 'You can't bend! You can't bend!' That translates to your ankles and keeps them still so you won't turn over and fall."

Off the ice, it seemed fitting that Colbert would become a huge Whoopees' fan. He showed up every night to ring his cowbell. He fell in love with the precision and speed of the sport.

"I never had been to see hockey before, but it was the most exciting game I had ever seen," he said. "It was a combination of all of the games, and every minute was action. From the beginning, I liked it better than baseball. Baseball was too slow."

Colbert found other ways to demonstrate his unwavering support besides his allegiance to the booster club.

He was unique in another sense.

He was black.

Although Macon boasted a large black population, it was not the traditional fan base that could be expected to support a hockey team. It was a foreign sport to most minorities. The Southern Hockey League had only one black player, Alton White of Greensboro.

Macon's most revered black athletes, the ones with the huge followings in the black community, had gained their reputations in other sports. John "Blue Moon" Odom, who grew up only a few blocks from Colbert, had just pitched for the Oakland A's in the 1973 World Series. Basketball great, Norm Nixon, was on his way from the playground courts of southwest Macon to the NBA. Julius Adams, Jim Parker, Tommy Hart, and J.T. Thomas left Macon and went on to become stars in the NFL.

In the third month of the Whoopees' season, Colbert retired after a twenty-five year career with the Macon Post Office. He had been foreman of collections and deliveries. Eight years earlier, he had become the department's first black supervisor.

His passion for hockey, his loyalty as a fan, and his ever-clanging cowbell caught the attention of the front office staff as the funk settled in. It was hard not to notice a black man in an almost all-white crowd. They could have called him "Spot."

A few days after reports began to surface that the Whoopees were skating on thin ice, a concerned Colbert wandered into the team's front office at 200 Coliseum Drive.

"He was disturbed about it and wanted to know what he could do to help," Buckley said. "We were immediately impressed with his enthusiasm."

Pinkerton didn't simply want to bottle that enthusiasm. He wanted to issue it a time card. "I understand you've retired from the post office," he told Colbert. "How would you like to work for the Whoopees?"

Colbert was flattered. And shocked. "I had offered to do volunteer work for the team, but I never dreamed of getting a permanent job."

Pinkerton announced that Colbert would carry the official title of promotions manager. His job duties would be to coordinate group attendance, create interest in a youth hockey program, work with the booster club, and help organize a summer youth hockey school.

At least Colbert didn't have to worry about keeping the day job. He had retired.

"I never really knew how much I was going to get paid," he said.

Getting paid would have been a new concept for anyone employed by the Whoopees.

When your skates aren't laced tightly, the ice can be so unforgiving.

'Houston, We Have a Problem'

"We were like family. We were all we had."

The words belonged to Bob Dupuis. The goaltender. The guy who protected the net.

While the players "owned" by WHA teams had a paycheck and a future, Dupuis was one of several Whoopees whose only future was the present. Although he would later play in the NHL, for now, Dupuis couldn't see past the Macon city limits. So, when the first paycheck bounced in December, did he see the writing on the rink?

"Oh, no," said Dupuis. "We were hockey players. We weren't the smartest. I think it was when the *third* check bounced that we started to figure it out."

One day the team was folding. The next day everything was OK. The *Telegraph* was becoming a print version of "Days of Our Whoopees." Pinkerton had become proficient at spinning a "Whoopees OK" headline into the sports pages.

"The players didn't want to quit," Pinkerton was quoted after a team meeting. "They all wanted to know how things were going with the franchise. They didn't even mention not getting paid."

Of course, Pinkerton didn't mention paychecks either. Nor did he sign any. Without money, roommates Gendron and Penasse were involved in their own budget talks. "We decided to just eat macaroni and cheese," said Penasse. "It was inexpensive, and it was one of Gendron's best dishes. We ate it just about every day. Georges had to fix it a lot of different ways."

In spite of "no pay" and learning to dance "The Macaroni," the Whoopees played well.

"We really thought that if we were good on the ice, somebody would buy the team, and we could continue," said Dupuis. "I thought that we would somehow finish the season."

In the middle of this soap opera that was being played out in the newspaper, the Whoopees defeated the league-leading Roanoke Rebels at the Coliseum, 5-4. It was one of KeKe's finest hours. With the score tied and only a minute remaining in the third period, Mortson scored the winning goal, his third of the game, a hat trick.

KeKe had publicly asked, even begged, for a big crowd. Only 800 seats were filled, and many of them were freebies.

"There were some people who had told me I couldn't play any more," Mortson said. "After getting a hat trick against the top team in the league, I wanted to call a few of those guys and have a word or two. Couldn't do it, though. The phones were dead."

Two days before Mortson's heroic effort, Southern Bell had cut the cord and filed suit for $2,418.72 in overdue phone charges. Buckley's leased car was also repossessed.

"That wasn't a big deal, really," said Buckley. "You don't need a car when you don't have to drive to the office."

Transportation was an issue though. Tapp was one of several players who had no way to get around. When he went to KeKe to ask for a raise so he could buy a car, KeKe offered him his old car.

"It was a '64 Pontiac that would bounce at stoplights because the shocks were gone," said Tapp. "When you went to the gas station, you would joke: 'Check the gas and fill the oil.' KeKe gave me that car. I heard he once went to the Houston Aeros to ask for a new car. He parked his old car in front of the arena until they got him a new one."

Meanwhile, it was official. The team's office telephone line was now on the wall in Buckley's apartment.

"The worse it got, the more people got together in each other's apartments out at Raintree," said Lauri Dupuis, Bob's wife. "Everybody would meet at someone's place to see what was going to happen next."

Bob and Lauri never will forget the day they walked to their favorite convenience store near the apartments. It had been almost two months since Dupuis had received a full week's pay check.

"Bob had been saving pennies for his little brother," said Lauri. "After so long without pay, we rolled up the pennies for a trip to the store to get whatever we could."

"When we went to the store, I always bought a twelve-pack of

Busch beer," said Bob. "It was my brand, and, no matter what else we bought, the twelve-pack went with it."

On this particular day, Bob and Lauri walked up to the counter with bread and a few other items. And the pennies. And no Busch.

"The guy at the counter looked at us and looked at the pennies," Lauri said. "And then he said, 'Is it really that bad?' We said 'yeah.'"

Without speaking, the storekeeper turned and put a few additional items in the Dupuis bag. Then he handed Bob his twelve-pack of Busch. "No charge," he said.

"I'll never, ever forget that," said Bob.

Enough was enough.

Voting twelve to two, the Whoopees decided not to play a game against Charlotte on January 18.

Pete Ford, who had just come to Macon from the folded Suncoast franchise, summed up the team's feelings.

"We can't play for nothing," Ford said. "We can't put promises on the table and eat them."

A picture on the front page of the *Telegraph* the next day showed Metcalfe on the ice, alone. The sight of the empty ice on a game night was unusual. The sight of empty seats was not.

"I dressed that night because of KeKe," said Metcalfe. "KeKe picked me up from the Greensboro team and believed in me. I owed KeKe Mortson as much or more than anyone else I ever played for because he gave me an opportunity when others didn't."

Metcalfe and Mortson had voted against the strike. Joining them in uniform was Ron Grahame, who didn't vote but said: "I really went out to play for KeKe. He's been good to me." Grahame's check was guaranteed by the WHA Houston Aeros.

Ron Morgan was under contract with Cleveland. He was told by the Barons' front office to honor the vote of the other players and proceed with the strike. He figured he had the day off, so he and several other players went to play golf.

"We headed down to the course with a couple of cases of beer," Morgan said. "We were almost finished with the round and with the beer, when someone came running to tell us the game was going to be played. We went straight from the golf course to the Coliseum."

It turned out to be just another rumor in a season of rumors. The game never was played, and Morgan was quite thankful for that.

"By the time we got to the rink," he said, "I don't think any of us could have stood up to play."

The face-off came and went and, with it, the only "forfeit" of the season. Without the required number of players dressed and ready to play, the rule book said you flunk out.

Dupuis believed KeKe took the strike vote personally. "He thought we were striking against him," said Dupuis. "So we made it plain that we were not doing this against KeKe. We were doing this against Pinkerton."

The strike worked. The players got some money, and, two nights later, this resilient team pounded Winston-Salem, 7-2. Mortson rewarded Metcalfe's loyalty by naming him captain. Metcalfe responded with a goal. The team played as if nothing had happened.

But something had happened. The player strike was the last straw for the parent clubs of the WHA. They began pulling out players. They paid their players to play, not strike. Houston called. Cleveland called. Players were shipped to teams that didn't strike.

"KeKe was doing everything he could to hold things together" said Bill Dineen, the Houston head coach. "He was pretty desperate for players, but he couldn't pay anyone. And yet, he had guys giving him 110 percent for, virtually, nothing."

The team roster dwindled to fourteen players, two below the usual minimum. Mortson told the media he might have to ask his trainer and assistant general manager to dress out.

Said Mortson: "Buckley might be worth a used net as trade bait."

Everyone laughed. For now.

'Now Playing...for One Minute'

Buckley usually wore a red blazer for home games. He constantly was on the move, checking tickets, making sure the media was taken care of, and following KeKe's signals. He wore about a dozen hats.

On this night, he wore a dozen on his back: Number 12.

"I should have been scared to death," said Buckley. "But KeKe had told me that if Roger Gibson, our trainer, and I dressed out we could buy a little more time. Roger and I would have done anything to help KeKe and the team. Anything."

"Anything" meant putting on a uniform on February 3. Ironically, the Whoopees were playing Buckley's old hometown team, the Greensboro Generals.

"KeKe told me he needed me to dress and sit on the bench so we would have enough players to officially field a team," said Gibson. "I was a little surprised when he told Billy to dress. But, we needed him, too. He could skate. Sort of."

For Gibson, being in uniform was not a big deal. Gibson had played professional hockey. He had enough hockey skills left from his playing days in Fort Wayne, Indiana, to skate a shift or two if the Whoopees needed him.

"I figured I owed it to the fans," said Gibson. "When I saw Billy skating in warmups, I was happy for him. He got to be a part of the roster of a pro hockey game. I said to myself: 'This man has got courage.'"

Dupuis had a different take on Gibson and Buckley in uniform.

"When I found out they were dressing, I had to assume they might play," said Dupuis. "I had seen Billy in warmups. I remember thinking that if I ended up in goal while Billy played, I was in for a long night and a lot of work."

When Buckley stepped onto the ice for the first time that Saturday night, there were cheers. No one had ever cheered while watching him do anything.

"Pure and simple, it was a thrill," he said. "I remember thinking: 'Just don't fall down.' We skated around the goal, and I remembered how much harder it was to skate wearing all that equipment. KeKe whizzed by and winked."

The crowd was calculated at 2,252. Not bad. Of course, the Atlanta Flames Booster Club was in town. So was the self-proclaimed "booster club without a team" from recently folded Suncoast. And, the Whoopee Booster Club would give away a new Ford Pinto after the second period as part of a promotion.

Buckley scored. During warmups.

As one of his practice shots slid, slowly, toward Grahame, the star goalie stepped out of the way. To the delight of Whoopee fans, he allowed Buckley's shot to trickle into the net.

But not everyone saw the humor.

"I remember thinking, 'My God, somebody is going to get killed,'" said Metcalfe. "Putting Roger and Billy out there was not a publicity stunt. It was just KeKe trying to make the team survive. I think he loved what he was doing, and he just didn't want to have to stop. I knew the size of the guys on the other team and the size of Roger and Billy. I was worried that one or both of them was going to get hurt. I wondered what the other team was thinking."

Wondering. And worrying.

"Protecting your goalie was one thing," said Metcalfe. "But trying to protect two of our players? That was unusual. Buckley looked like he would need a lot of protection."

Yeah, and maybe an ambulance. Of course, you can't get hurt if you don't play. Getting on the ice during the game was not even remotely being considered by Buckley, who came off the ice and shared bench time with the injured Brian Tapp.

After Tapp watched Buckley skate in warmups, he turned to him on the bench and said. "I'm glad we're not paying you to play."

As the third period began to wind down, KeKe looked up at the clock and then at the Whoopees' fans across the rink. He could hear them yelling for "Buckley." It was a great crowd, but a disappointing game. The number of fans in the seats was the good news. The number of pucks in net was the bad news.

The game was lost. With only two minutes remaining, players stirred around the bench collecting their equipment for the short skate to the gate that would lead them back to the dressing room.

Suddenly, KeKe's shrill voice pierced the air.

"Buckley! Get over here!"

Never one to disappoint a crowd, KeKe was about to oblige them one more time. He yanked at the gate, and suddenly Buckley was on the ice. The fans yelled their approval.

"I'd like to think I charged out there ready to do battle," said Buckley. "But I know that wasn't true. Somebody had to have pushed me."

The push probably came from KeKe. Buckley poured onto the ice during a shift change. He skated from the blue line to center ice, and, as he was turning to attempt to follow the play, KeKe summoned him back to the bench.

"When I came off the ice, I was in shock," said Buckley. "It probably was best that I didn't have to think about it. KeKe said as I passed him: 'Now, you're a pro.'"

Although he was on the ice for no more than forty seconds, the Hockey Register, the bible of hockey players, credited him with one minute of professional playing time.

"That was KeKe," said Metcalfe. "He just wanted to give Bill that special memory. And just look at what a memory it has become."

The St. Valentine's Day Massacre

It was Valentine's Day.

Hugs and kisses, candy and flowers, and a whole lot of whoopee. In a few weeks, America's sweetheart, Doris Day, would turn 50. In Macon, Georgia, hearts were being broken.

"I'll always remember it as the St. Valentine's Day Massacre," said Buckley.

The city's four-month romance with hockey was over. It was February 14, 1974. Nine days before the season was supposed to end, Buckley and other team officials began making phone calls to round up the players.

Sudden death. End of game. Whatever will be, will be.

The first cars in the parking lot that day had government stickers on the doors. Agents from the Internal Revenue Service moved in and seized everything from aspirin to hockey sticks.

Instead of going through pre-game drills for an upcoming game against Greensboro, the sound of electric drills could be heard in the bowels of the Coliseum.

The doors to the locker room were being padlocked shut.

"They weren't big men at all, those IRS agents," said KeKe. "Physically, our hockey team could have picked them up and thrown them out the door. But the law is the law. They put a seal over the dressing room door. Our guys told me: 'KeKe, you can take that and rip it up.' And I said: 'I never could fight 212 million Americans, and I'm not about to start now.'"

Gibson was one of the first to get a call. He had the keys to the dressing room.

"I had the home jerseys in my car because I had taken them out to be dry-cleaned," Gibson said. "I turned them over to the IRS. Right then, I said: 'This has to be the saddest day of my hockey career.'"

The players lined up at the locker room door and, one by one, were allowed into the room to gather their personal belongings. Everything else became property of the IRS.

"We were supposed to pick up any equipment that was ours, but when you are a goalie, you don't *own* your equipment," said Dupuis.

The U.S. government didn't know that. "KeKe came to the door with these IRS people and said: 'OK, come on in and grab whatever belongs to you,'" said Dupuis. "I went in, but none of it belonged to me. I don't even know why I was in line. I just kind of looked at KeKe, and he said: 'Sorry you don't have a bag for all of your equipment.' I had nothing, and I walked out with *everything*."

Ellis Pope showed up from the *Telegraph* to gather information for a story on the upcoming Greensboro game. Instead, he found the doors locked. There would be no game, only a shutout.

He looked for Pinkerton, but the owner was nowhere to be found. Somebody told him Pinkerton was dead. "Well, he wasn't," said Pope. "Nobody dies on the IRS. But the Whoopees did."

The bills were stacked too high. So were the odds. Since December, the team had been living on credit cards and borrowed time. There had been thirty-six roster changes. While trying to stick fingers in the dike, the Whoopees had simply run out of hands to plug the holes.

Pinkerton was very much alive. He was fleeing north on Interstate 75, the same ribbon of concrete that had steered him to Macon. Those were the times in his pre-Whoopees past when he couldn't get that crazy Doris Day tune out of his head.

His dream of owning a hockey team was busted into a million pieces. He gripped the wheel of his car and tried to hang on.

"It was the saddest drive of my life," he said. "Boy, that was tough. I was really depressed. People that do away with themselves when they are really having problems, I understand what they're going through."

The end had been in sight for so long. So why was this so incredibly tough? Maybe it was because it was like a terminally-ill patient. No matter what the prognosis, no matter the difficulty of the treatment and the dim prospects of recovery, the best medicines are always faith and hope.

It was time to swallow the bitter pill. "The sad thing about that last day was that the parking lot attendants came in and told me they felt like it probably would have been one of our biggest crowds of the year," Buckley said. "I've always been left with the feeling that Macon was going to respond. They were turning out to see if something could be done. Unfortunately, it was too late."

At the mayor's office, Ronnie Thompson also tried to get a puck-sized lump out his throat. "I considered the Whoopees an industry, and you're always sad when it doesn't work out," Thompson said. "What saddened me was that they left in such a hurry. We didn't have a chance to say good-bye. They were here, and then they were gone."

"We were close because of everything we went through," said Dupuis. "I played on a lot of teams where the guys couldn't stand each other. Everybody got along on this team. I guess we still believed. We had a good nucleus, and we were doing well. I really thought we would somehow finish the year, make the playoffs, and go on from there."

Dupuis gathered the equipment he now "owned" and headed out the back door of the Coliseum. Even though the paychecks had been AWOL since Christmas, the spirit of the team still seemed to hang over the building.

"Those players loved the game of hockey," said Ellis Pope. "It was more than a business. Their love of the game transcended any monetary gain. They would give up their bodies for the sheer pleasure of victory. Sure, some of them had dreams of making the NHL. But most of them knew, down deep, that this was their last hurrah on ice."

At the loading docks, a group of maintenance workers sat dejected. They never had seen hockey until the Whoopees had brought life and laughter to the Coliseum floor 125 days earlier.

They had gotten attached. Now the plug had been pulled.

"They were dejected and so were we," said Dupuis.

The door was shut behind them. It was over. Said Dupuis: "Then we started worrying about how in the hell we were going to get home."

Welfare Farewell

The Whoopees were dead. The booster club knew it. The struggle to keep the team in Macon was over. The effort to help penniless players get to their next destination was not. So the boosters threw a party for the players at the Hilton. They brought covered dishes and kegs of beer.

Geri Frank wore a black dress.

"I was in mourning," she said. "These were exceptional young men who went down with the ship."

The remaining players soon would be leaving for cities far from Macon. The boosters wanted one last chance to say good-bye. The hotel ballroom had been rented for the bon voyage. In one corner, a glass fishbowl was ready to collect money to pay for gas, food, and bus tickets.

A microphone was set up in the front of the room. It was to be a night of farewells. And welfare. "All the guys with the parent clubs had gone," said Tapp. "The players left were the ones with no place to go. I went up to the microphone and talked about how I was going to miss the city. I really, really enjoyed playing in Macon."

Many of the players who attended the booster club party were sleeping on the floor of their apartments. Their furniture had been repossessed. Because some of the apartment managers were threatening eviction for unpaid rent, boosters offered to have hockey players move into their homes.

"The boosters were great," said Don Giesebrecht. "What they did for the players that night was something I'll never forget. The rumors had been changing every day. KeKe obviously was kept in the dark. It was sad because it was the last night a lot of us would ever see each other."

It also was the last time Buckley would ever see KeKe.

While hats were being passed and heads bowed in reverence, KeKe signaled for Buckley to follow him toward the kitchen door. In the kitchen, KeKe turned and looked Buckley in the eye. His own eyes were wet and red. He reached into his wallet and pulled out a personal check he had written earlier that day.

Buckley tried to refuse the check.

"Take it, Billy," KeKe said. "Don't make me cry."

KeKe returned to the party. Buckley stayed in the kitchen and opened the folded check. It was for $500. In the lower left corner, KeKe had written: "For loyalty."

It took Buckley a while to return to the party. Now he had something in *his* eyes.

The beer flowed, along with the tears.

"The way the ties were being severed, there was a sense of incompletion," said Dupuis. "The end of a season is always sad. Guys you've been with all season are going their separate ways. If you have a losing season, you have no one to blame but yourselves. We had a helluva hockey team. We had some talent. We were winning but we couldn't finish. Everything was out of our hands. There was just no closure."

As the evening wore down, each player and many of the boosters took a turn at the microphone.

Finally, it was KeKe's turn to speak. It would be his last public appearance in Macon. "He stood at the mike and started talking about how he was sitting around his apartment on one of the two rented chairs he had left," said Lauri Dupuis. "And everyone laughed."

Everyone needed to laugh.

KeKe spoke of his fondness of Macon and how the boosters were among the best group he had seen in his many years of hockey. He talked about his players and the job they had done and how much he appreciated their staying with him at the end. Everyone could feel KeKe's pain at having to let go of a team he had worked so hard to build.

"It was devastating to him," said Carol Lavery, the wife of the coliseum manager. "He was intense and devoted. I think Macon and the idea of this team in the South was something he was determined to make work. He would have done anything he could to make that possible."

Suddenly, "anything" and "everything" were not enough. And, it hurt.

Still at the microphone, KeKe paused. As any hockey player will tell you, the best way to get rid of pain is to inflict pain. KeKe focused his anger and delivered.

"You know," he began, "I've heard of sex maniacs in my time, but Jerry Pinkerton takes the cake for screwing eighteen people at once."

The room roared. There was no rebuttal.

Pinkerton was nowhere to be found.

The guy who used a song as his inspiration to start the team had chosen not to stick around and face the music at the end.

Another Season, Anyone?

Doug Bell was convinced hockey could make it Macon.

"Given the right organization and the right backing, the Whoopees would still be here," he said in late February.

Bell was a transplanted hockey nut who had volunteered to be the official scorer for the Whoopees. During the job interview, Pinkerton learned that all Bell wanted was a seat at the scorer's table. No money. Bell was hired instantly.

After the season was cut short, Bell said what many Macon fans wanted to hear.

"There is no reason we can't have hockey next season."

Another season? No reason? For Macon Whoopee?

Buckley didn't ask Bell to repeat himself. He had heard all he needed to hear.

"Having just lived through the wrong way to run a sports franchise, I figured I had learned enough to make it go," Buckley said. "If we could just get local investors interested. I was excited."

With all of eight months of so-called professional experience, Buckley figured he was now "ready" to do it right.

What Bell and Buckley wanted to do, with the blessings of the booster club, was simple. Local ownership. Better organization.

A prospectus entitled "A Professional Hockey Franchise In Middle Georgia" was created by a special committee of the booster club. Individually, and in groups, it was presented to community business leaders with hopes of finding some deep pockets.

The prospectus admitted the problems of the now-defunct Whoopees and highlighted how the new organization would adhere to the Southern Hockey League's rule of "seventy percent local ownership."

Other items on the "we won't do this again" list included no more free ticket deals. It was estimated that 25 percent of the fans at each Whoopees game were freebies. No more high payrolls. The plan called for lower-cost players. No more "exclusive" training camps. Training camp would be in Macon.

The booster club listed itself as the biggest single asset to the new owners. The boosters claimed to have a ticket-buying fan base of 1,260 per game and 240 season tickets committed for another season.

Buckley called KeKe, who was back home in Canada.

"He never said I was crazy," said Buckley. "I think he was still as gung-ho as I was. He wanted Macon to have a team. I hoped it would help when I got his commitment to come back to Macon and coach the new team."

The nine-page proposal included promotions, plans to sell the popular "Mr. Whoopee" T-shirts, a plan to request that the Whoopees earn a percentage of the gate receipts from away games, new ticket prices, and a schedule that did not go one-on-one with God. There was also a line-item budget.

"Now *that* was different," said Buckley. "I had worked for a hockey team from the Fourth of July through Valentines Day, and the first budget I ever saw was a month after the team folded!"

One of the booster club goals was to buy the equipment that was to be auctioned off by the IRS in early April. Bell arranged for a local businessman, who did not want to be identified, to purchase the equipment.

The auction made the front page of the morning paper. "It was a wake," said the *Telegraph* story. "Almost like having someone auction the belongings of your deceased friend. They even sold the sweat of KeKe Mortson."

For Buckley, the auction is a vivid memory and a turning point. He had taken a job at a liquor store to help pay his bills and was living with some booster club members. He put forth the same effort and enthusiasm for a new franchise as he had in his Whoopees position.

"I remember picking up KeKe's hockey sweater, No. 99, at the auction and thinking that things suddenly were different," said Buckley "The newspaper writer described it perfectly. It was like a funeral. As I looked around and saw all those sweaters, I didn't see numbers. I saw names. It was then that I realized that, while there might be another season, it couldn't possibly be the same."

Until that morning on the IRS auction block, Buckley wasn't really trying to get another hockey team in Macon. He was trying to get *his* hockey team back in Macon. He remembered how he hadn't been a hockey fanatic when he took the job. He suddenly knew that, while he still hadn't become all that enamored with hockey, he did love the team.

In spite of the revelation at the auction, Buckley and the boosters pressed on in their efforts to secure the cash for a new team. Unfortunately, the long-suffering public death of the Whoopees was a too-recent memory. Most of the money in Macon already had sat through a deathbed plea from Pinkerton.

It was just too soon to see past all the scary red ink. Good business people do not run toward something that has just failed.

Bell didn't have any money. The boosters had a lot of things, but money wasn't one of them. And Buckley may have been the first graduate of Guilford College ever to lose money his first year in the work force. As tax time rolled around, he told friends that his revenge against the IRS was that he got to use the "short" form.

Reality set in at a special booster club committee meeting.

There was no money. There was no more time.

It was like deja vu. All over again.

High Stickin' With the Angels

"No one dies until I get back home in the spring."

That was a strict order from KeKe Mortson when he left home every autumn for another hockey season.

"He was not going to stop playing to come to a funeral," said his brother, Dennis. "We had the same set of instructions each season."

KeKe was in control. Of his hockey. Of his family. He was even in control of his immortality.

Or, so he thought.

The cancer arrived suddenly and decisively in mid-1995, like a game that cannot be rescheduled. Always a fighter, KeKe skated in the face of death. He played his last hockey game only forty-one days before his funeral.

After all of those "No one dies until..." speeches, KeKe broke his own rule.

"He died in the middle of winter," said Dennis. "In the middle of hockey season, in the worst storm we had during that winter. He did exactly what he told us never to do."

KeKe used to tell people there was only one way to get to North Bay. You had to fly to Toronto, take the train fifty miles north into the bush, and then travel the rest of the way by dog sled.

"I don't think a dog sled would have helped you get to KeKe's funeral," said Jane Mortson, KeKe's widow. "The church was filled, but there were so many people who just couldn't make it. The weather was that bad. A lot of people called to tell us they just had to turn back."

As he stepped to the pulpit on December 11, 1995, to speak at his brother's funeral, Dennis couldn't help but grin at the crowd that filled the pews. It was the coldest day of the year and the worst snowfall since 1965. He told them of KeKe's annual directive.

"I'll betcha he's just smiling like hell at the inconvenience he's put us all through," said Dennis.

There was laughter. At a funeral.

"I will not eulogize my brother," said Dennis. "I find that I cannot even share with you the memories we had as a family. Those were our moments, our memories, our special time. If you are here today, you have your memories of being with KeKe. Those memories are better to have than any words I can give. Treasure those moments, and recall them often."

In the spring of 1998, at KeKe's home in North Bay, a small gathering of family, friends, and former players watched as lockers filled with pieces of his twenty-two seasons were opened for the first time since KeKe's death. It would have been his birthday. He would have been sixty-four.

Inside the chest were newspaper clippings from the years in Baltimore and Seattle.

There were programs from Hershey and pucks from Dallas.

There was at least one photo with each of the nineteen teams for which he played. But no one uniform had enough colors to outfit him. Golf had Chi Chi. Hockey had KeKe.

One item was missing from the chests. His Number 99 Macon Whoopees hockey sweater. It was upstairs in his closet.

"He practiced in it all the time," Jane said. "He had a lot of sweaters from a lot of different teams, but that's the one he always wore. He loved it."

There were more holes than thread. In all of the games he played after leaving Macon, Number 99 always managed to find a place in his equipment bag. It was a proud memory. As the chests were emptied, there were more photos, more memories, and more stories. His youngest son, Jay, remembered the many nights KeKe's teammates would drop by and laughter would fill the house until dawn. KeKe had finished his career with 348 goals and 218 stitches. When his skin was slashed in a game between the North Bay Old-Timers and the Pembroke Pot Bellies, a veterinarian playing for the other team stitched him up.

Although KeKe had been elected to the North Bay Sports Hall of Fame in 1989, he would not allow himself to be officially inducted. "When I'm dead...then you can do it," KeKe had said. He was inducted in March, 1996.

Those who visited KeKe's house and explored the "treasure chests" learned of KeKe the husband, father, brother, player, teammate, and coach. But, most of all, they learned of KeKe's character. The same KeKe who could have an entire arena of opposing fans ready to kill him was the KeKe who, for years, regularly washed the family's clothes and mopped the floors.

The same KeKe who would drop the gloves for a fighting penalty claimed "Misty" as his all-time favorite song. He especially liked the Johnny Mathis version.

The same KeKe who ran rugged conditioning drills and a grueling training camp was the KeKe who once taught a group of young hockey players attending a camp the method of properly spitting through their masks. When confronted by a fellow coach, KeKe exclaimed, "They gotta learn the fine points of the game!"

The same KeKe who once claimed that all of his penalties were "good ones" is now buried near a rise of cedar trees in a cemetery on the outskirts of North Bay. He rests beside his first wife, Clara, who died in 1982.

A wrought-iron hockey stick protrudes from the ground. If the graveyard had a penalty box, KeKe would be in it for perpetual high sticking.

As the chests were emptied, it was obvious that the Whoopees occupied the greatest amount of square footage inside. There were photos, clippings, pucks, and programs. Everything else was in his heart.

"KeKe was extremely sentimental about Macon," said Dennis. "In my mind, I can't even picture that the team lasted only four months because of the emphasis KeKe placed on the Whoopees. When you'd listen to KeKe, you would have thought he had spent his entire career in Macon, not just for a short time."

Dennis would listen to his older brother talk of his time with the Whoopees in what KeKe sometimes called the "Lover's League."

"When he would talk about the players and the city, KeKe's face would shine, and he would smile," said Dennis. "All his memories of Macon and the Whoopees were pleasant. He had a lot of fun with that team."

A few feet from the room where KeKe died, Jane Mortson sat

at a piano and played the song, "Makin' Whoopee." She remembered December 8, 1995; the day KeKe died.

"You know, KeKe really wasn't looking forward to getting old," said Jane. "He had told that to his sons, Lindsey and Jay, and he got his wish."

Apparently, sixty-one was old enough for KeKe. He had been diagnosed with skin cancer. Jane thinks he spent too much time sitting in the backyard in the summer sun with no shirt, enjoying a beer. Or two.

As the inevitable end of his life became obvious to both KeKe and Jane, their thoughts turned to the past. They talked about a lifetime of "seasons."

"Of all the places he had played hockey, Macon was his favorite," Jane said. "It truly was the time of his life—his favorite time in the game."

During one of those final, personal conversations, Jane asked if KeKe had any regrets as he looked back over his life.

"He thought for a moment, looked up at me and said: 'Just one,' " Jane said. "He said: 'I regret not having $10,000 down there in Macon to pay all those players who played for me without getting paid.'"

Soon, with that one regret, he was gone.

To say Jane Mortson is a bit of a gambler is an understatement. Remember, now, she *married* KeKe. Nowadays, she plays the lottery. She plays because she promised she would.

"Before KeKe died, he made me promise," said Jane. "And, when I win, I am to get in touch with all those players and pay them."

She keeps an up-to-date list of player phone numbers handy. She plans to keep her promise if and when those numbers come in.

Even though he's now high stickin' with the angels, KeKe's favorite team remains his Macon Whoopees.

Number 99.

Forever and ever.

22. Homecoming 1998: Buckley walks to center ice at Double Rinks in North Bay, Ontario, Canada—25 years after KeKe and the Whoopees skated here In training camp. (Photo by Ed Grisamore)

23. Last Skate: KeKe Mortson wore these skates during the last hockey game he played—only forty-one days before his funeral in North Bay. (Photo courtesy of Jane Mortson)

24. KeKe is now buried near a rise of cedar trees in a cemetery on the outskirts of North Bay. A wrought-iron hockey stick protrudes from the ground at his gravesite. (Photo by Ed Grisamore)

Say, Didn't You Used to Be?

The biggest "save" Ron Grahame ever made was for... Budweiser.

"Yeah, it's kind of funny to admit it," he said. "But that 30-second beer commercial gained me more notoriety than my entire playing career."

Considering Grahame's career, when you say Budweiser, you've said it all.

The year following his stint with the Whoopees, Grahame was named MVP of the WHA championship Houston Aeros team. Then it was on to Boston, where he played for one of the six original NHL teams, the Bruins.

"It was fun playing for Boston," said Grahame. "I got the chance to play a period of hockey in the Stanley Cup playoffs. We were playing in Montreal. Of course, the best part of the memory is Montreal didn't score on me."

Then it was on to tinsel-town and another NHL franchise, the Los Angeles Kings.

Although his play in L.A. didn't produce a lot of great memories, it did give him the opportunity to do his now-famous beer commercial in December 1982.

"My hockey career was about over. I really didn't play all that well in L.A., and, at that time, no one wanted me," Grahame said. "There was a guy I played with in Los Angeles named Murray Wilson. He heard about a casting call for a commercial that had something to do with hockey. We didn't know exactly what."

Murray and Ron went to the casting call and found the advertising people were looking for a goalie to play a part in a TV ad.

"I went into a little room where they had set up a makeshift goal," said Grahame. "They gave me a 2x4 piece of wood and asked me to act like a goalie and make some saves. Well, that was pretty simple for me."

Within a few days, Ron got a call to see if he would be interested in traveling to Portland to film a beer commercial.

"Budweiser was competing with Miller Lite, and this was their first stab at promoting their new light beer," said Grahame. "I said 'sure.'"

He was in Portland for three days filming the commercial. "We spent about a day and a half on the ice doing the things you do in a hockey game as part of the commercial," said Grahame.

The commercial did not require Grahame to speak, but he did have to produce "the look."

"We had been told up front that there would be no speaking part," he said. "What they wanted was hockey action, and they had to have players, coaches, fans—all of the elements of a hockey game.

"The theme of the commercial was 'Bring out your best,'" Grahame said. "I got scored on, and the coach was upset with me. He glared at me from the bench, and I knew he was unhappy with the way I played."

Through his mask, Grahame gave the coach the "I'll do better" look as he stalked around the goal waiting for play to resume. He gave his stick a determined slap.

"After looking at the coach, I played great," said Grahame, who didn't allow another goal for the rest of the commercial. "It's really the story of the non-verbal connection between a coach and a player—and the commitment that follows. With his look, the coach is saying 'Do better,' and with my look, I'm saying, 'I will,' and I did."

The commercial was an instant success. "It turned out pretty good for me," said Grahame, who heard about the commercial everywhere he went. "It ran nationally for quite awhile, and they used it during the 1983 Super Bowl."

Did the commercial make him rich?

"Oh, no," he said. "I paid some bills with what I earned. But it was mostly just a lot of fun doing it."

Now, as he reminisces about his career, does the fact that he did a national beer commercial come up?

"Oh, sure," he said. "All the time. But then, so does the fact that my pro career started with the Macon Whoopees."

The 'Ball' Game and Extra Innings

In retrospect, football fans must have snickered when they reviewed the roster of the new sport in Macon. The players were the size of water boys. The roster was dotted with vital stats of 5-foot-9 and 174 pounds.

But one name usually got their attention.

Blake Ball: 6-3, 230.

Now, *that* was more like it.

They probably were even more impressed when they found out Ball once had served as a police officer in Toronto. And that the linebacker-sized Whoopee had played two seasons of Canadian football.

"On hockey teams you've got some little guys who can't take care of themselves," said Ball. "My job was to take care of them — to make sure no one pushed them around. I did that job well."

Blake Ball played the role of "offensive defenseman" perfectly. He was an extra-large in a locker room of mediums. His role was that of protector, defender and intimidator. He worried players on other teams, because, when Blake Ball hit you, he left his business card: *pain.*

"He was a gentle giant," said KeKe. "He could play the tough role, but he was really a nice guy."

Ball's efforts resulted in penalties for slashing, elbowing, tripping and high sticking. "I hit only one player over the head with my stick in my career," said Ball. "And that's only because he hit me first. I got cheap calls from the officials, but I think that was because of my reputation."

Ball's reputation was well-earned. While most hockey players averaged less than two minutes per game for penalties, Ball's average was five. Commit the crime. Do the time. There were those who said the penalty box was Ball's second home. "I've lost a few fights," said Ball, smiling. "But, I've won most of them."

Blake Ball was the first hockey player with whom Choo Choo Lynn's wrestling fans could relate. Not surprisingly, Ball traveled the professional wrestling circuit in Toronto during the off-season. "I wasn't supposed to do it," said Ball, whose hockey contract prohibited him from such summer activities. "But, like those guys who wrestled in Macon, I wore a mask, so no one could tell who I was. I also used different names."

Translated: He was never caught in the act.

In 1977 however, Blake Ball was *asked* to act. Ball made a brief appearance as a menacing defenseman in the movie, "Slap Shot," starring Paul Newman. "I had played in Johnstown (Pennsylvania) with the Jets," said Ball. "One of the players on that team had a sister who actually wrote the book. When it came time to shoot the movie and they thought about a 'tough guy' to play the role of the enforcer, they thought about me."

As a result, Ball auditioned and got the part in the popular hockey comedy. Ball enjoyed working with Newman and still enjoys seeing the actor from time to time. So, at 6-3, 230 pounds, was there anything Blake Ball was afraid of during his Whoopees days in Macon? Oddly enough, yes. Ball found Mayor Ronnie Thompson's tank and the famous "shoot to kill" philosophy a bit scary. "I just didn't know what to think when his tank rolled up," said Ball, laughing. "I really didn't mind getting out of Macon with all that shooting going on. The mayor's method of dealing with crime in those days made me a little nervous."

Ball also found that his first experience in the South kept him on guard for fear of making a mistake out in public. "I loved the people of Macon, but some of the customs down in Macon were different," said Ball. "When I was out and about in the city, I was really conscious of what I said, what I did. I just didn't want to say or do the wrong thing."

The *same* guy who set team and league records for penalty minutes did not want to offend anyone! Today, Ball is semi-retired and dealing with a few health issues as a result of one of those monster hockey hits. He works for a construction company from his home in Grand Junction, Colorado. He operates heavy equipment including bulldozers.

The gentle giant is still pushing things around.

Where They Are Now

Ace Azar is retired and living in rural Montgomery County, Georgia.

Bill Ashmore works for Dessau Realty in Macon and hasn't been to a hockey game since the Whoopees left.

Jack Billman is retired and living in Macon. He is an off-ice official for the new Whoopee hockey franchise.

Bob Barnette is retired as Central High School's band director.

Harley Bowers retired as executive sports editor of *The Macon Telegraph* in August 1996 and was instrumental in getting the Georgia Sports Hall of Fame built in Macon.

Bill Buckley is senior vice president and national sales manager for Momar, Inc., a chemical manufacturer in Atlanta.

Vernon Colbert is retired and a former Macon City Councilman. He was an off-ice official during the Whoopee's first year back in Macon in 1996-97.

Cliff Corley is an optician living in Columbia, S.C.

Bill Dineen is retired from hockey but cheers on his beloved Detroit Red Wings from his home in Lake George, New York.

Doris Day, a veteran of 42 films, lives in Carmel, California, and is active in the Doris Day Pet Foundation.

Bob Dupuis is a 15-year veteran with the North Bay police department, where he serves as a 911 dispatch operator. **Lauri Dupuis** is a home health care specialist.

Bill Elder is a popular morning disc jockey for WAYS-FM in Macon and still has the old Eddie Cantor recording of "Makin' Whoopee."

Bob Fierro is president of EQUIX Biomechanics of Lexington, Kentucky, a thoroughbred consulting firm. He lives in White-stone, New York, and is publisher of *New York Thoroughbred Observer*.

Geri Frank is an accountant in Macon.

Georges Gendron owns an oil distribution business in Auburn, Maine. After leaving school to follow her husband's hockey career, **Gwin Gendron** is about to receive her college degree.

Georgette Gendron still lives in Sturgeon Falls, Ontario.

Roger Gibson is a stone mason and brick layer in Espanola, Ontario.

Don Giesebrecht works with a family-owned soft drink distributor in Petawawa, Ontario.

Ron Grahame is an assistant athletic director at the University of Denver.

Talisa Hanson is employed at Rosa Taylor Elementary School in Macon.

Doug Harvey, a 10-time NHL all-star, died in 1989 at age 65.

Wayne Horne is retired due to health reasons and lives in Cornwall, Ontario.

Dan Jaskula works for television station WGNM in Macon.

Steve Johnson is pastor of Mabel White Memorial Baptist Church in Macon.

Johnny Jones works at the U.S. Post Office in Macon.

Kim Lander works as a lab technician at Dental Prosthetics in Macon and is a goal judge for the new Macon Whoopee hockey franchise.

Bill Lavery retired from coliseum management and lives with his wife, Carol, in Jacksonville, Florida.

Leroy's whereabouts are unknown.

Bruce Lockerbie is a consultant in Stony Brook, New York

Don Lockerbie is a design consultant for athletic stadiums. He lives in Chapel Hill, North Carolina.

Choo Choo Lynn retired from both the railroad and as a local wrestling promoter in 1990.

Suzanne Markert is director of the preschool program at Ingleside Baptist Church in Macon.

Norm Metcalfe is director of business development and marketing for an engineering and contracting firm in Ontario.

Tony McMichael lives in Winter Haven, Florida, and is graphics editor for *GolfWeek* magazine.

Ron Morgan is a partner for PLM Group, a printing design and distribution firm near Toronto.

Dennis Mortson is a semi-retired financial planner and lives in Englehart, Ontario.

Jane Mortson retired after teaching elementary school for thirty-six years and lives in North Bay.

Tedd Munchak worked as an entrepreneur in Atlanta until his death in August 1995.

B.C. Musick is retired as a bus driver and lives in Macon.

Richard Nixon resigned as President just six months after the Whoopees folded and moved to San Clemente, California. He died in 1994. History has never proven he wasn't buried in his Whoopees shirt.

Mike Penasse is back on the Ojibway Indian reservation in Garden Village, Ontario. He owns a building supply and septic tank disposal business.

George Penasse is deceased.

Jerry Pinkerton lives in New York City, where he works as a financial planner.

Bobby Pope is athletic director at Mercer University and was part of the ownership group of the Macon Whoopee for the 1997-98 season.

Ellis Pope works in the development office for the college of veterinary medicine at the University of Florida.

Al Rycroft is a regional manager for Ace Hardware and lives in Penticton, British Columbia.

Brian Tapp owns and operates a travel agency in Kelowna, British Columbia.

Ima Jean Tharpe is retired and living in Macon. Her sister, Thelma, is deceased.

Ronnie Thompson is a mental health administrator in Macon and moonlights at a local funeral home. In June, 1998, he received his college degree from Western Illinois University at the age of 63; he completed his college studies through correspondence work.

Score One for the Afterlife

It was a beautiful Sunday afternoon in early February. The sun was out. There wasn't a cloud in the sky.

As cars began to fill the rows around the Coliseum, a familiar figure began to stride across the parking lot. He walked through the doors and looked around. Just for old time's sake.

It was then that Jerry Pinkerton—arriving unannounced and traveling incognito—watched a hockey game in Macon for the first time in twenty-four years.

It was 1998. Time, it seemed, had healed all the old wounds. A lot of them, anyway. He was quiet at first, then the memories began to rush the net that had been carefully guarded by a deep sense of loss. He rubbed his eyes and began to talk. Hockey was back.

He looked below at the ice. This was not the Macon Whoopees. This was the Macon Whoopee, a second-year franchise that had dropped the 'S' but added the "$" in bringing a hockey franchise back to this central Georgia city.

For Pinkerton, the surroundings seemed so familiar, yet so drastically changed. The Coliseum had been renovated. A new ice floor had been put down. The old "chicken wire" around the rink had been replaced with modern plexiglas.

The logos on the Macon uniforms had been changed. The fans in the stands were more knowledgeable about the game. Everything had a new look, a new feel.

Hockey, it appeared, was going to make it in Macon after all.

Pinkerton leaned across his seat. "I'll tell you something. When I thought of that name, I had no idea what was going to happen," he said. "I just got carried away with the name."

If there is an afterlife in hockey, the Macon Whoopees certainly had one.

The memory, and the name, were frozen in time over the next two decades. Sometimes, the song would be played, and someone would remember there was once this certain hockey team.

Bob Wright certainly remembers. He bought all the Whoopees' equipment. Wright, who ran a sporting goods store in North Bay, learned about the used equipment from KeKe not long after the team folded. All the Whoopees' worldly possessions had been seized by the IRS and bought at an auction by a local entrepreneur. Wright took off for Macon in his wife's station wagon and paid $2,500 for enough shoulder pads, shin guards, and sweaters to equip sixty players.

"I bought everything but the skate sharpener," said Wright. "We had fifteen bags stuffed in that station wagon. It was quite a load. When we got to the (Canadian) border, they just waved us through. They didn't even ask for a bill of sale, which is a good thing because I didn't have one."

Wright sold most of the equipment out of his garage, but kept enough to outfit a team. KeKe played for one year with that team—the Sturgeon Falls Canadians—minus the Whoopees logos. A local businessman then bought the uniforms, and a junior league team called the "Little Butchers" skated in the Whoopees threads for several more years.

Those uniforms, just like the team itself, became the answer to a trivia question. For years after the team had died and dashed off to those giant dasher boards in the sky, people from all over the country would call or write to inquire about Macon Whoopees' pennants, pucks, T-shirts, and bumper stickers. The locals lucky enough to own Whoopees' memorabilia were smart enough to realize their value as collector's items.

Historians and writers would ask questions about the intriguing team and its short history. The Whoopees, it seemed, had the power of preservation. They were embedded in local folklore and eulogized by such nationally known sports writers as Dave Anderson of *The New York Times*.

In 1985, the Macon Whoopees topped the list of the "60 All Oblivion Unusual Nicknames" in the book *Sports Hall of Oblivion*, by Chuck Hershberger. The Sports Hall of Oblivion is located in Where, Michigan, and the unusual nickname list also included the New Westminster Salmon Bellies, the Chattanooga Choo-Choos, and the Southern California Bangers.

In 1991, a quote from a fictitious Macon Whoopees player named James Nasal appeared in a national print advertisement for Reebok. Dennis Vaughan, a copy writer for the Boston advertising agency Hill-Holiday, admitted the "Nasal" was a joke. But he was inspired to include the flesh-and-blood Whoopees. As a youngster, he would listen to his father, a hockey announcer on a Medford, Mass., radio station, spin tales about the team.

Neither Vaughan nor his father ever saw the Whoopees play. But they both were intrigued by the name.

"I get tired of the Lions, Tigers, and Bears—oh, my!" he said. "Whoopees is one of the great nicknames of all time."

So great, in fact, that in Vaughan's estimation, the only two names that ever have come close to rivaling the Whoopees belong to two baseball teams—the Toledo (Ohio) Mudhens and Kissimmee (Fla.) Astros.

Kissimmee's name was later changed to the Osceola Astros. The Kissimmee Astros were found to be rather offensive—if certain syllables were accented.

In many ways, the Whoopees could be credited with being at the forefront of a national trend of clever nicknames for professional hockey teams. Nearly a quarter of a century after their demise, the Whoopees begat a revolution of fun-loving names.

Orlando now has the Solar Bears, Huntsville the Channel Cats, and El Paso the Buzzards. Hockey has ushered in the Jacksonville Lizard Kings, Wheeling Nailers, Austin Ice Bats, Minnesota Moose, and Bakersfield Fog.

Much of the credit for the resurrection of hockey in Macon has to go to Lou Corletto, a former assistant general manager of the Washington Capitals. Not only did Corletto get an assist for the reincarnation of the Whoopees, but he also dusted off the old Southern Hockey League and was appointed its commissioner.

Corletto, too, was infatuated by the Whoopees' nickname and approached two old friends, Julian Lerner of Charleston, S.C., and Bob McIntyre of Dalton, Georgia. He convinced them to fork out the $100,000 franchise fee and return a team to Macon in 1995.

Lerner and McIntyre later backed out, citing the high costs for ice-making equipment and an unsatisfactory lease agreement with the city. The ice-making apparatus was a necessity. The Coliseum had long since removed the piping and other ice equipment.

Corletto tried, without success, to entice other potential investors to Macon. He was determined that the city was going to have hockey again for the 1996-97 season and admitted that the league's survival hinged on the novelty and attraction of the Whoopees' unique name.

By September, he had found his men—Richard Ray and Pat Nugent—and by March, they announced that they had purchased the franchise.

Nugent's resume included a stint as general manager of the Hampton Roads (Va.) Admirals of the East Coast Hockey League, as well as a baseball player personnel director for the New York Yankees, Chicago Cubs, and Atlanta Braves.

"Nearly every city in the South is getting a team," Nugent said. "Hockey is on a high cycle right now....If I didn't think we could be the No. 1 draw in the league, I wouldn't be here."

It wasn't all smooth skating. In June, 1996, just five months before the start of the season, the Florida franchises folded. By the following month, Macon joined another expansion club, the Columbus Cottonmouths, and an SHL holdover—the Huntsville Channel Cats—in the more competitive Central Hockey League.

The Whoopee hired John Paris, Jr. a former coach of the Atlanta Knights, as head coach of the Whoopee. In December, 1996, the team signed a seven-year lease with the city, ensuring that there would be Whoopee in Macon through the 2003 season.

The new Macon team made the decision to drop the "S" from the end of the nickname, but keeping the idea of the name intact proved to be smart thinking on the new owners' part.

Said Nugent: "We would have made a great mistake if we had not chosen to keep the name. It's like this team never left here twenty-two years ago."

The new franchise, however, did select a new logo—a fig leaf with the words "Macon Whoopee" across the front. The leaf motif was replicated to make the Whoopee outfit closely resemble the uniforms worn by the Toronto Maple Leafs. The fig leaf also is indigenous to Georgia with more than two dozen varieties.

Of course, the symbolism was lost on most people that designer figs were the first apparel worn by Adam and Eve, who incidentally have been credited with discovering whoopee. Soon, the joke around Macon was that Adam had once been a hockey player at the Madison Square Garden of Eden.

From the start, it was obvious that management was going to have fun with the nickname. Like Nixon, President Bill Clinton was given a Whoopee shirt on a campaign stop in Macon in 1996. It wasn't long before Clinton was having some political troubles of his own.

They invited actress/comedian Whoopi Goldberg to throw out the first puck on opening night. She had to decline because of a previous commitment, but she autographed three pucks and sent them back to Macon. She asked the team to sign one of the pucks and return it to her for her collection.

Although the franchise went through several front-office changes and suffered through a slow start for the first six weeks of its inaugural season, the new Macon Whoopee were successful in their first two years on Macon ice.

The team averaged 3,641 fans per game during its initial season and 3,767 in 1997-98. The team made the playoffs both years, and made good on its promise to go out and "kick some ice." In March, 1997 a group of local investors bought a majority of the club, and the franchise signed a contract with a local radio station to broadcast the games.

In the summer of 1998, the ownership group was considering ditching the fig-leaf logo in favor of a more marketable and fan-friendly mascot.

Yes, they were the Whoopees, but they might as well have been the Pioneers. Or the Trailblazers.

"They were a concept that was before their time," said John Shoemaker, general manager of Riverside Ford, which has remained a major sponsor. "We just weren't ready for hockey in 1973."

Pinkerton doesn't point fingers.

"People did support the team," he said. "We just didn't know what the numbers should be because there never had been hockey here before. We didn't have the money to make it go. You can blame anybody you want. But you can't blame the people."

What the original Whoopees organization lacked in experience, it made up for in enthusiasm. It didn't work because of timing and circumstances, not because there was a shortage of effort.

"I cried about it then. But, when I look at it now, I'm absolutely dumbfounded that we went down to Macon and did what we did," Pinkerton said. "We didn't know we were going to have to pay the police, the parking, the Coca-Cola guy, the Zamboni driver. We had no idea."

He said he wanted to own a hockey team partly because of his love of the sport and, admittedly, partly because of ego.

"Let me tell you something about professional sports. You see yourself on television or in the newspaper, and somebody comes up and says: 'Can I have your autograph?' When I look back on it, I think you really do buy it for ego," he said. "It got me on New York TV and on 'The Dating Game.' Who the hell knows George Steinbrenner if he doesn't own the Yankees?...I guess when I either do an American Express commercial or go to my grave, at least it can be said that I once owned the Macon Whoopees."

Buckley still looks back at his Whoopees days with wonder. "When something fails, you have a tremendous sense of loss," he said. "For a lot of years, I think I took it personally that the Whoopees didn't make it. I felt that if I had done a better job and had known more about what I was doing, we could have made it. I have since been assured that wasn't the case. We didn't have the money, and it was just a matter of time."

He still gets a little choked up when he hears a recycled version of "Makin' Whoopee" like the one recently played on Cadillac commercials. He keeps an old Southern Hockey League puck as a conversation piece on the desk of his Atlanta office.

His three sons all have worn his old Whoopees' Number 12 sweater at different times as part of their Halloween costumes. They remain fascinated by their father's former life, hearing the old war stories and marveling at how it all came to be.

"You know what they say about everyone having a defining

moment in their lives? Well, the Macon Whoopees were my turning point," Buckley said. "I'm convinced there's not a thing I'm doing now that I would be doing if it hadn't been for the Macon Whoopees. It changed my life forever. I'm now living a dream. I'm doing exactly what I enjoy doing and working with wonderful people. I have the greatest wife in the world and a beautiful family. And none of it would have happened if I hadn't made that drive to Macon."

Like others, he was thrilled to see hockey return to Macon in 1996. He didn't rush out and buy the first ticket, though. He was afraid he might jinx the new team.

"I'm vindicated now," Buckley said. "They wouldn't have the name if it hadn't been for the original group. I feel so good for the fans now that supported us back then. I share that great feeling that Macon now has a successful hockey team. Only through our failure could that have happened."

Macon Whoopees Final Statistics

Player Name	GP	G	A	Pts	PIM
Cleland "KeKe" Mortson	59	24	51	75	135
Al Rycroft	53	38	31	69	18
*Gary Williamson	58	25	33	58	38
Ron Morgan	51	25	27	52	101
Ray Adduono	40	14	38	52	95
Jean Fauteux	53	17	33	50	35
Don Giesebrecht	56	19	27	46	31
*Norm Metcalfe	41	14	22	36	28
*Mike Penasse	60	11	22	33	170
*Norm Schmitz	59	5	27	32	26
Norm Cournoyer	25	11	15	26	65
Wayne Pushie	54	9	15	24	61
*Georges Gendron	49	5	19	24	33
Pete Ford, Suncoast	31	3	11	14	8
Macon	26	1	6	7	12
Totals	57	4	17	21	20
Jim McMasters	24	1	15	16	19
Wayne Horne	12	7	8	15	6
Steve Johnson	17	2	9	11	10
Terry Flaman	29	1	10	11	66
Glen Grigg	13	4	4	8	0
Jack Stanfield	3	6	1	7	4
Brian Tapp	34	1	4	5	141
Ed Hoekstra	2	0	5	5	0
Bart Fahlgren	8	1	2	3	28
Ron Grahame (G)	46	0	3	3	4
Blake Ball	15	2	0	2	69
Derek Kuntz	10	0	2	2	12
*Andre Lajeunesse	7	1	0	1	0
Rene Levasseur	8	0	1	1	6
John Vaudry	1	0	0	0	0
Glenn Paraskevin	1	0	0	0	0
Bob Hesketh	1	0	0	0	12
Bill Buckley	1	0	0	0	0
Ray Gibbs (G)	7	0	0	0	0
Bob Dupuis (G)	19	0	0	0	2
Totals		244	430	674	1227

*Did not finish season in Macon, but did finish with another team in the same league.

Southern Hockey League

Final Standings 1973–74

	G	W	L	T	P	GF	GA
Roanoke Valley Rebels	72	53	19	0	106	366	244
Charlotte Checkers	72	44	27	1	86	309	227
Greensboro Generals	71	33	37	1	67	285	310
Winston-Salem							
Polar Twins	72	26	44	2	54	283	363
*Macon Whoopees	62	22	38	2	46	244	290
*Suncoast Suns	31	9	22	0	18	123	176

*Did not complete season